MEL BAY'S Tenor Banjo Chords

MEL BAY

This book was created in response to many requests for a catalog of tenor banjo chords arranged in a photo-diagram form for maximum ease in understanding and playing.

Cover photo courtesy of Liberty Banjo Company, Bridgeport, Connecticut.

1 2 3 4 5 6 7 8 9 0

INDEX OF CHORDS

THE CORRECT WAY TO HOLD THE TENOR BANJO

THIS IS THE PICK

Hold it in

this manner →

firmly between the

thumb and first finger.

Use a medium

soft pick.

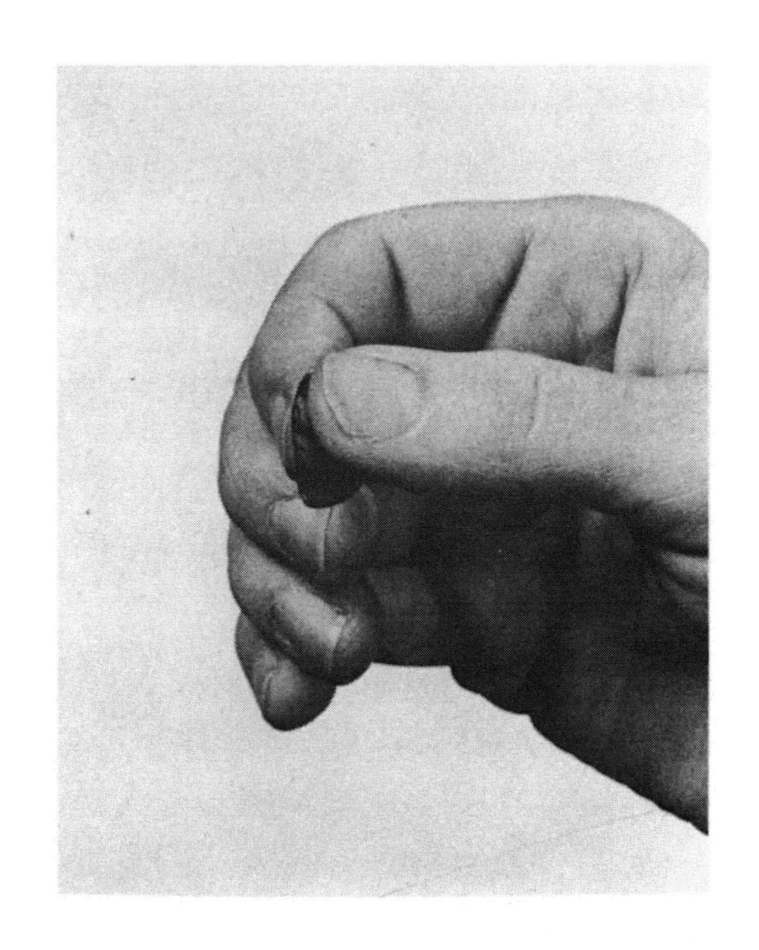

THE LEFT HAND

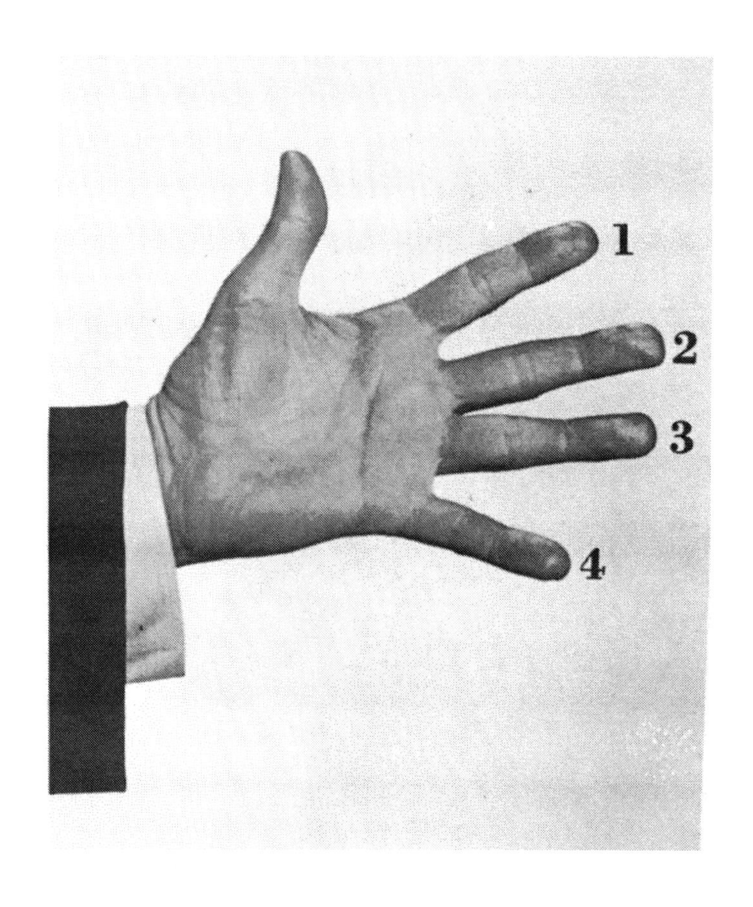

Practice holding the Tenor Banjo in this manner.

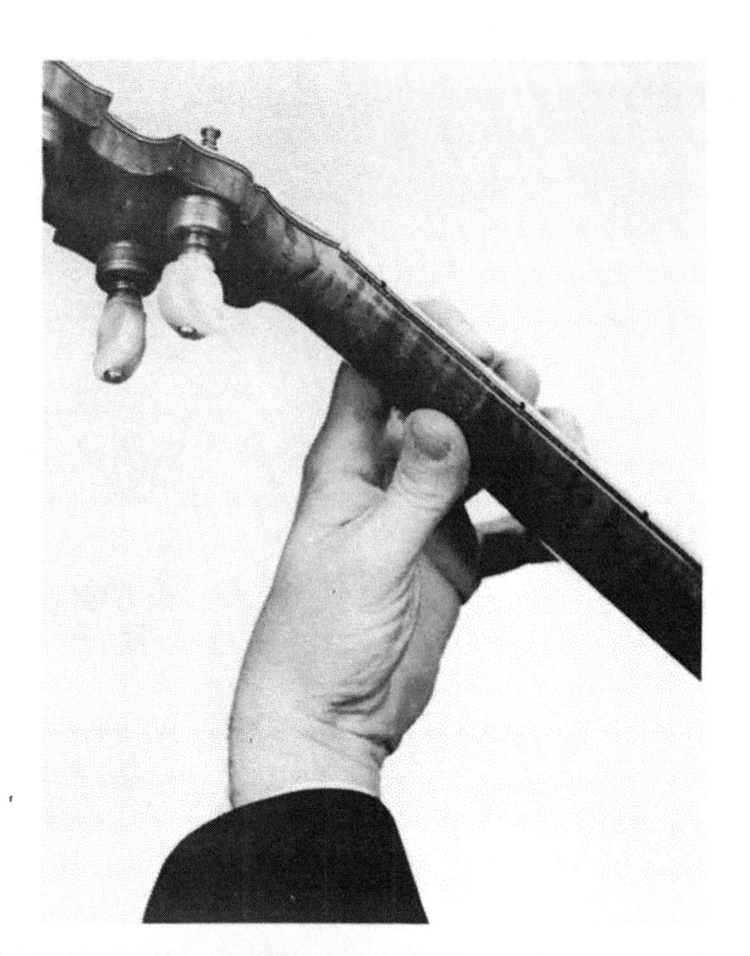

Keep the palm of the hand away from the neck of the instrument.

THE FINGERBOARD

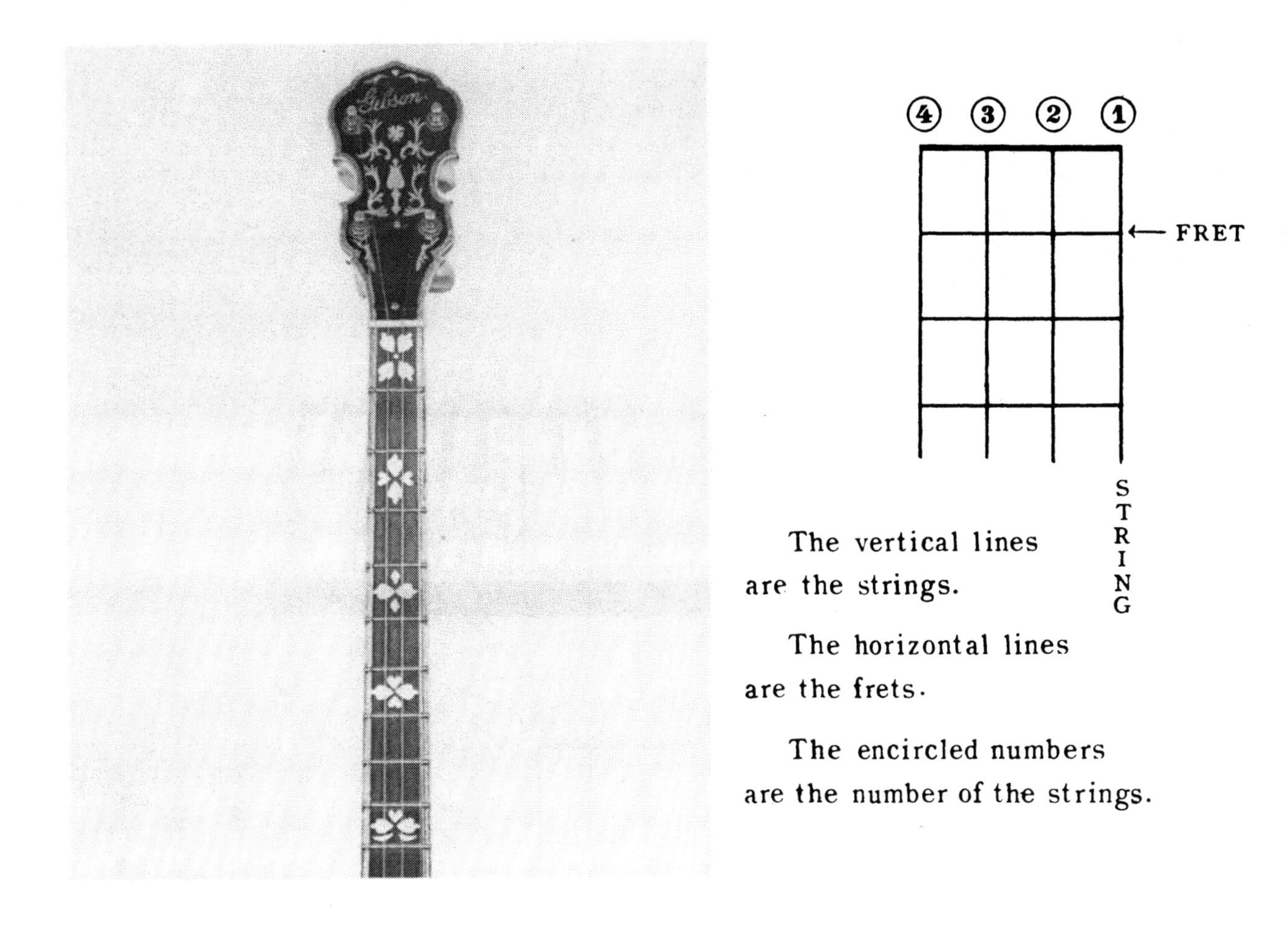

The vertical lines are the strings.

The horizontal lines are the frets.

The encircled numbers are the number of the strings.

Striking the Strings

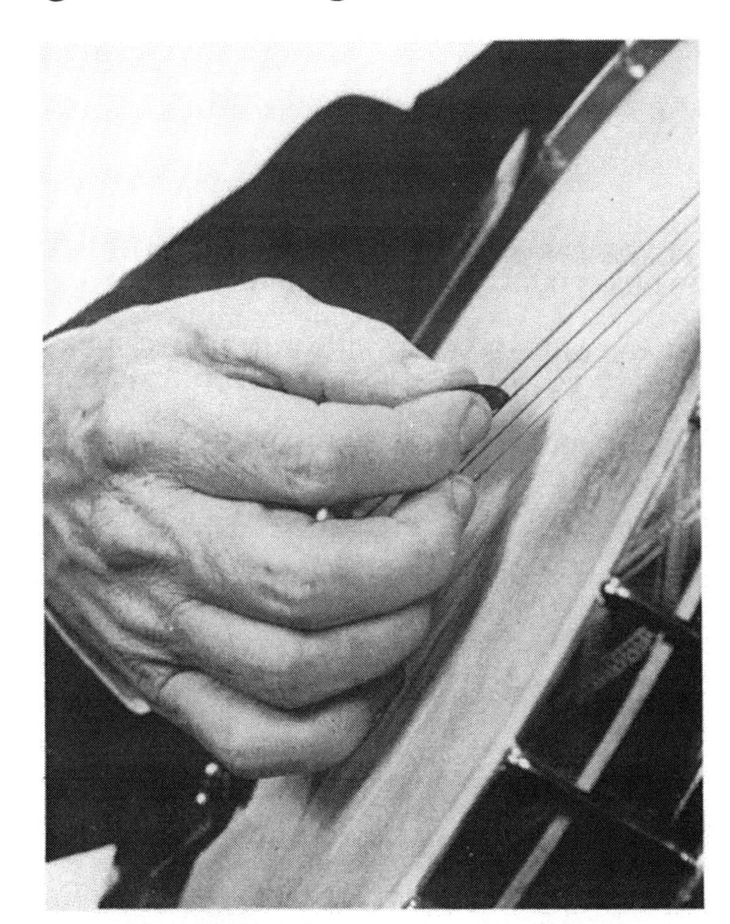

⊓ = Down stroke of the pick.

Tuning the Tenor Banjo

First String . . . . A ①
Second String . . . . D ②
Third String . . . . G ③
Fourth String . . . . C ④

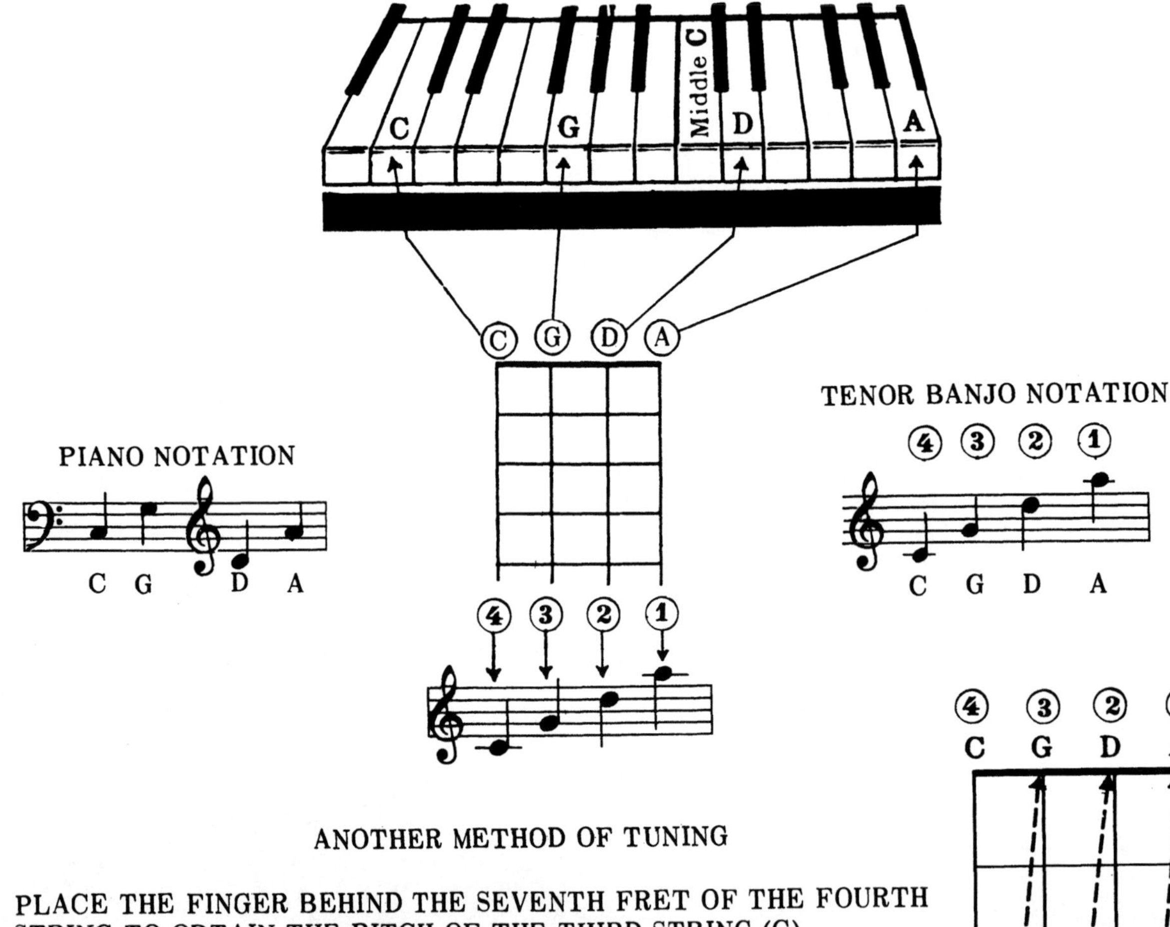

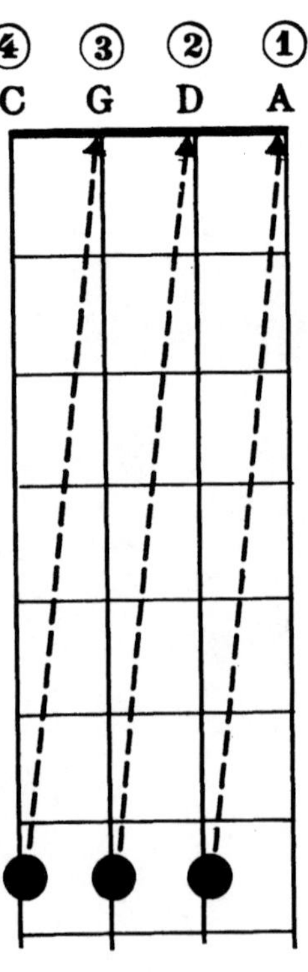

ANOTHER METHOD OF TUNING

PLACE THE FINGER BEHIND THE SEVENTH FRET OF THE FOURTH STRING TO OBTAIN THE PITCH OF THE THIRD STRING (G).

PLACE THE FINGER BEHIND THE SEVENTH FRET OF THE THIRD STRING TO OBTAIN THE PITCH OF THE SECOND STRING (D).

PLACE THE FINGER BEHIND THE SEVENTH FRET OF THE SECOND STRING TO OBTAIN THE PITCH OF THE FIRST STRING (A).

Pitch Pipes

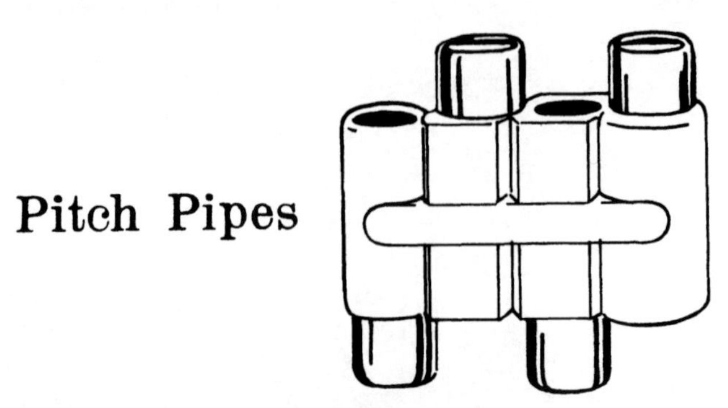

PITCH PIPES FOR THE TENOR BANJO (CELLO) MAY BE PURCHASED AT ANY MUSIC STORE. EACH PIPE WILL HAVE THE CORRECT PITCH OF EACH TENOR BANJO STRING. THESE ARE AN EXCELLENT INVESTMENT.

THE MAJOR CHORDS

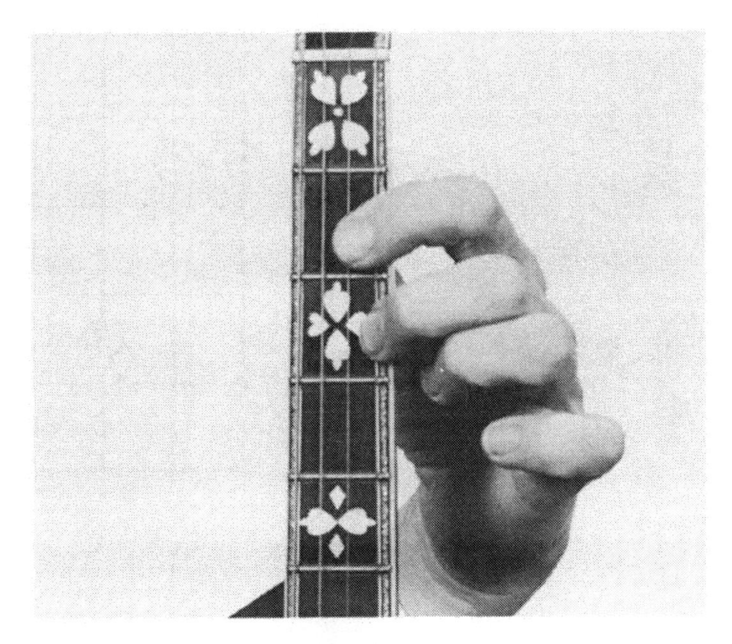

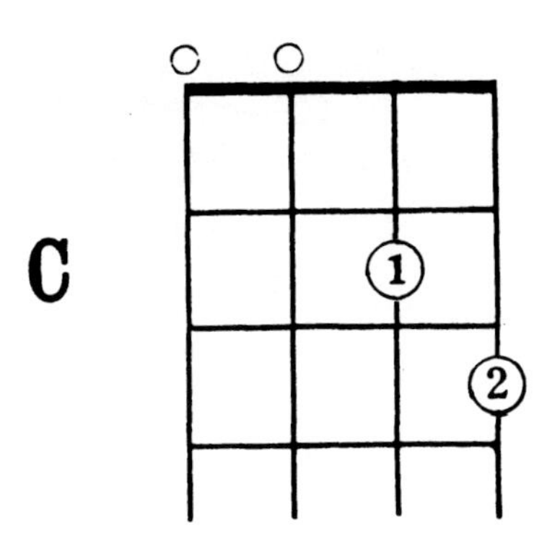

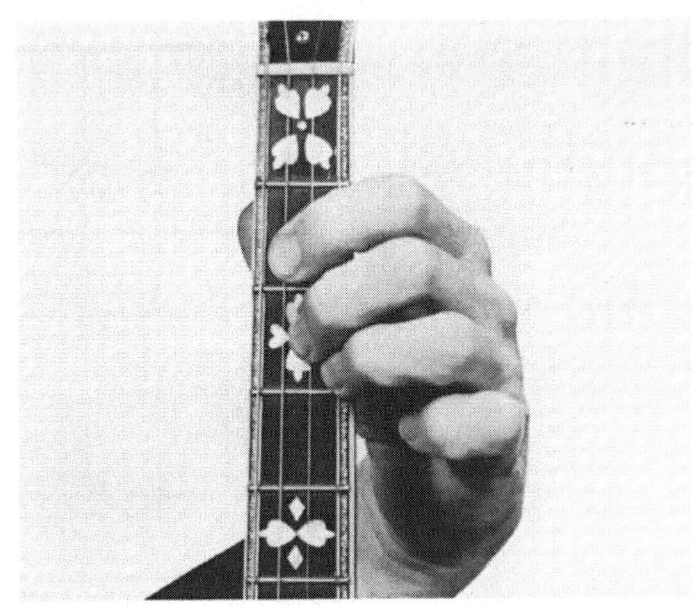

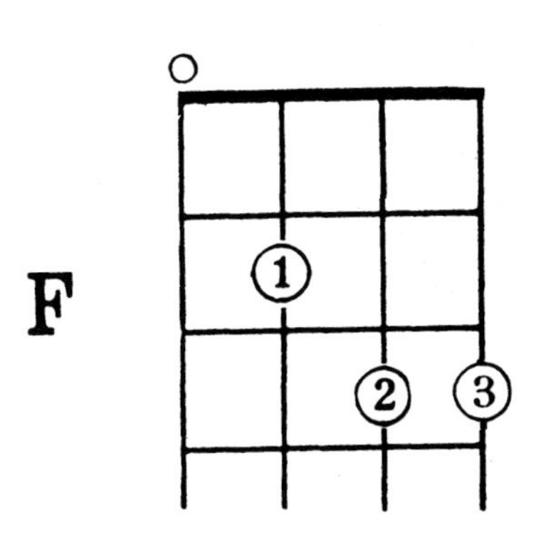

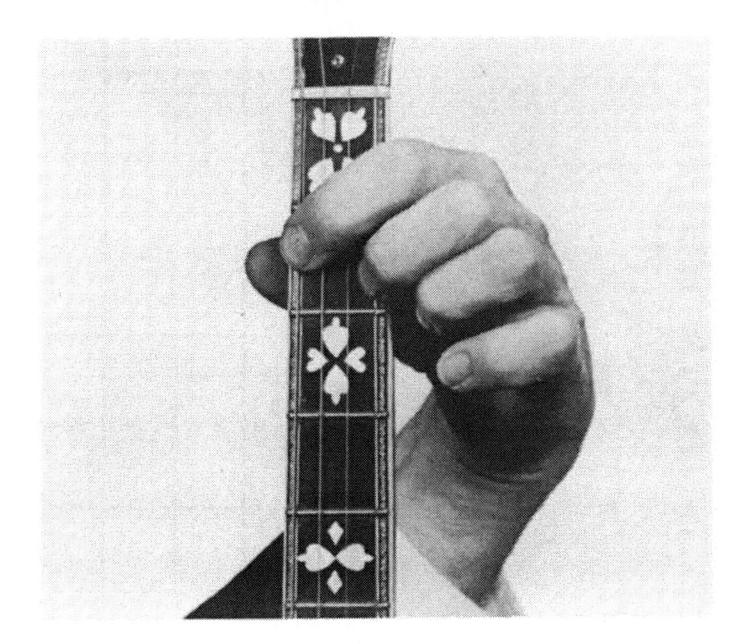

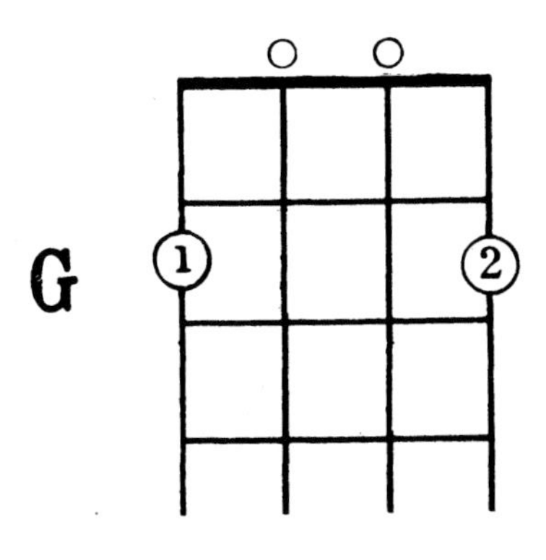

THE MAJOR CHORDS

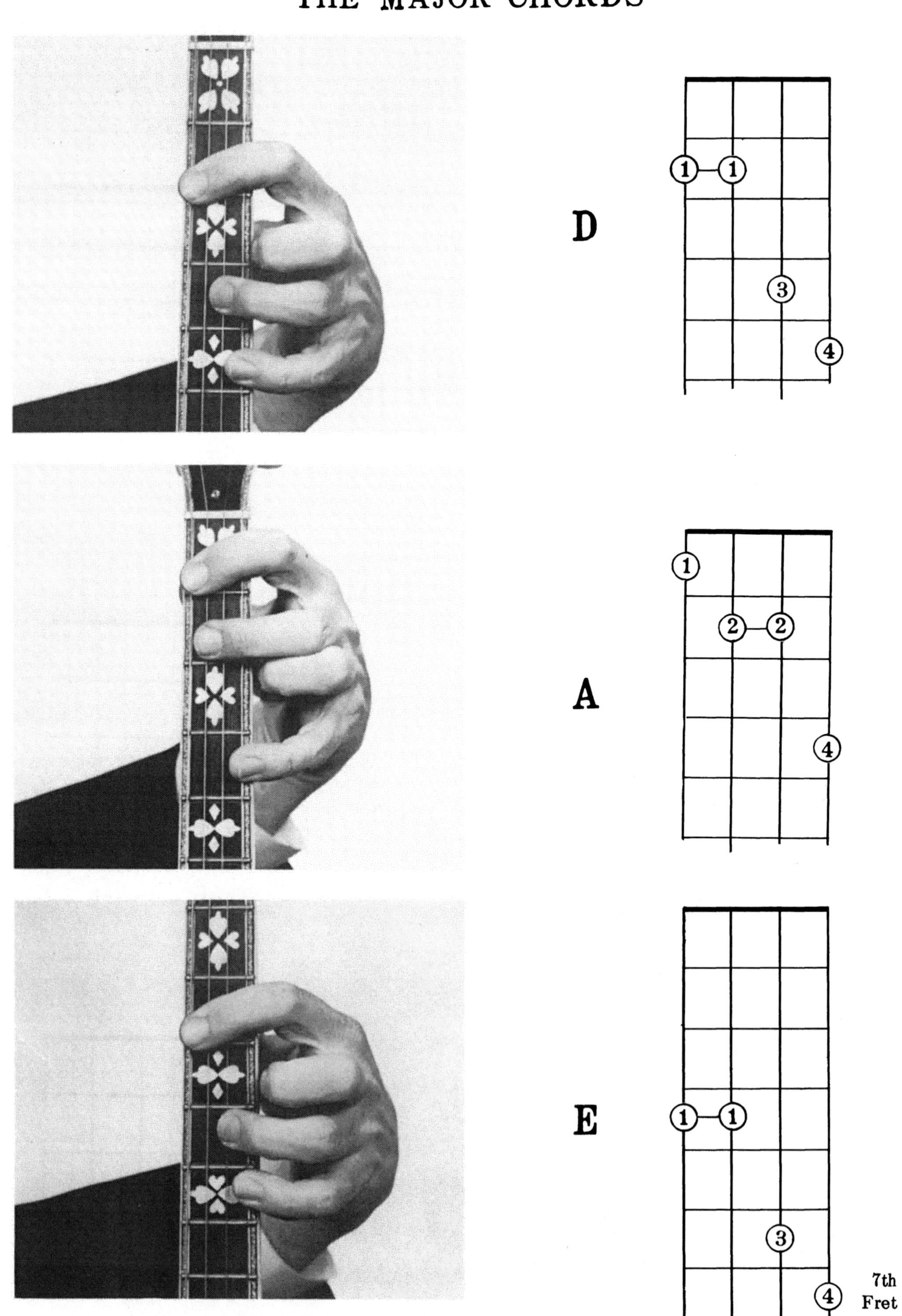

THE MAJOR CHORDS

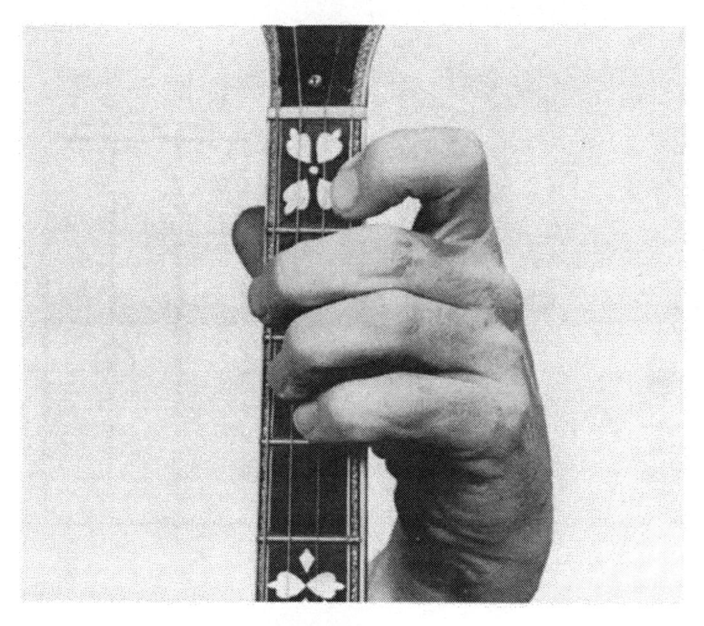

B♭

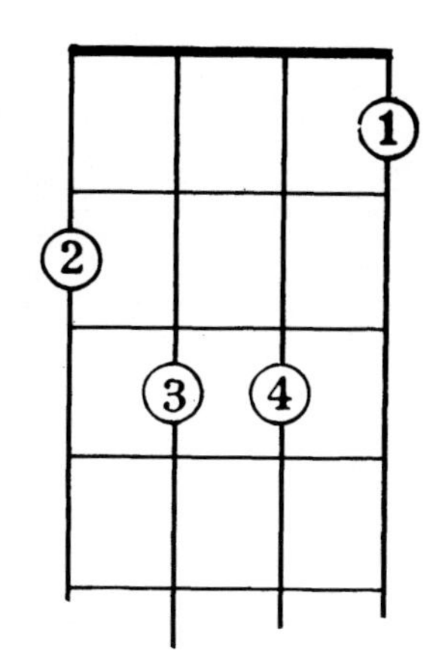

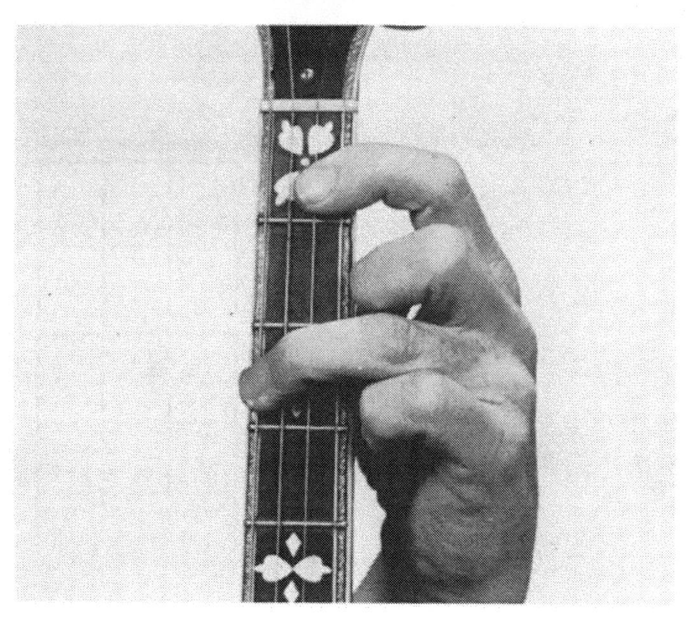

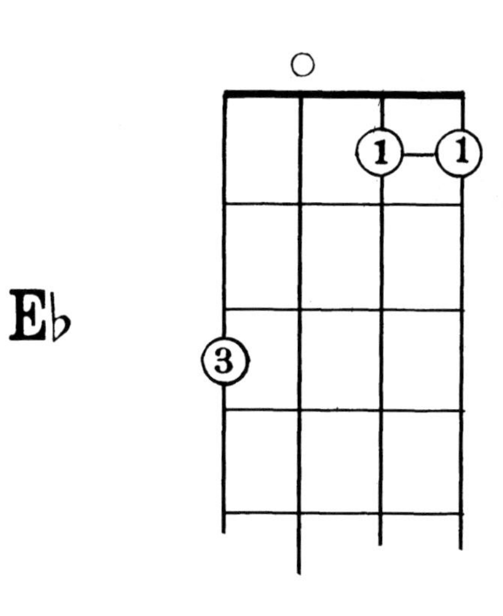

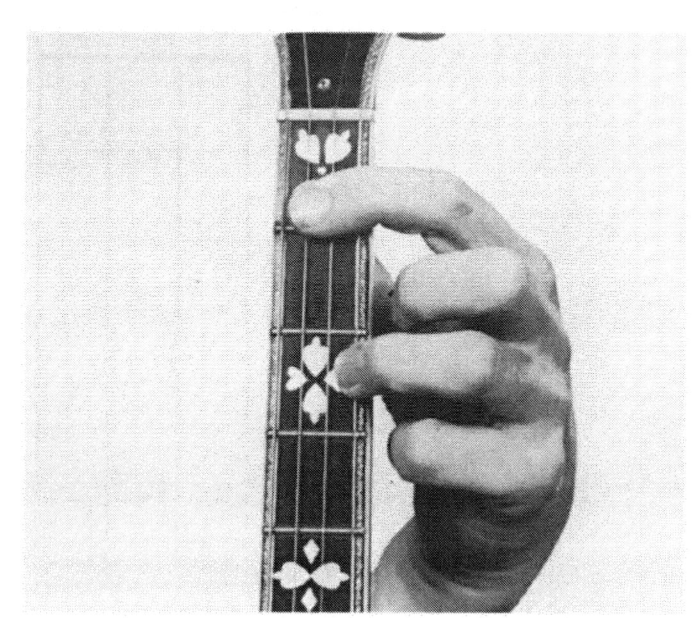

A♭

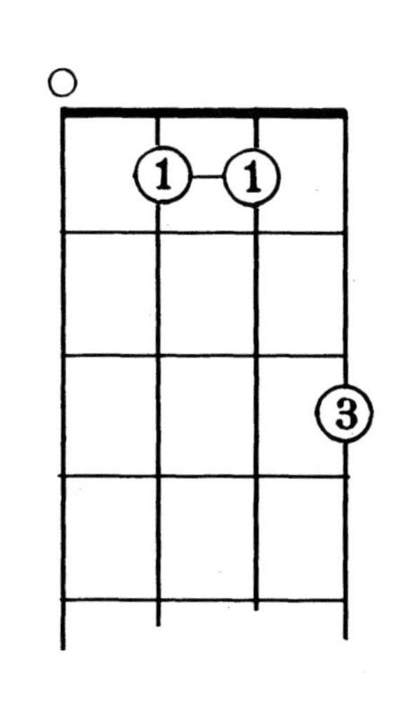

THE MAJOR CHORDS

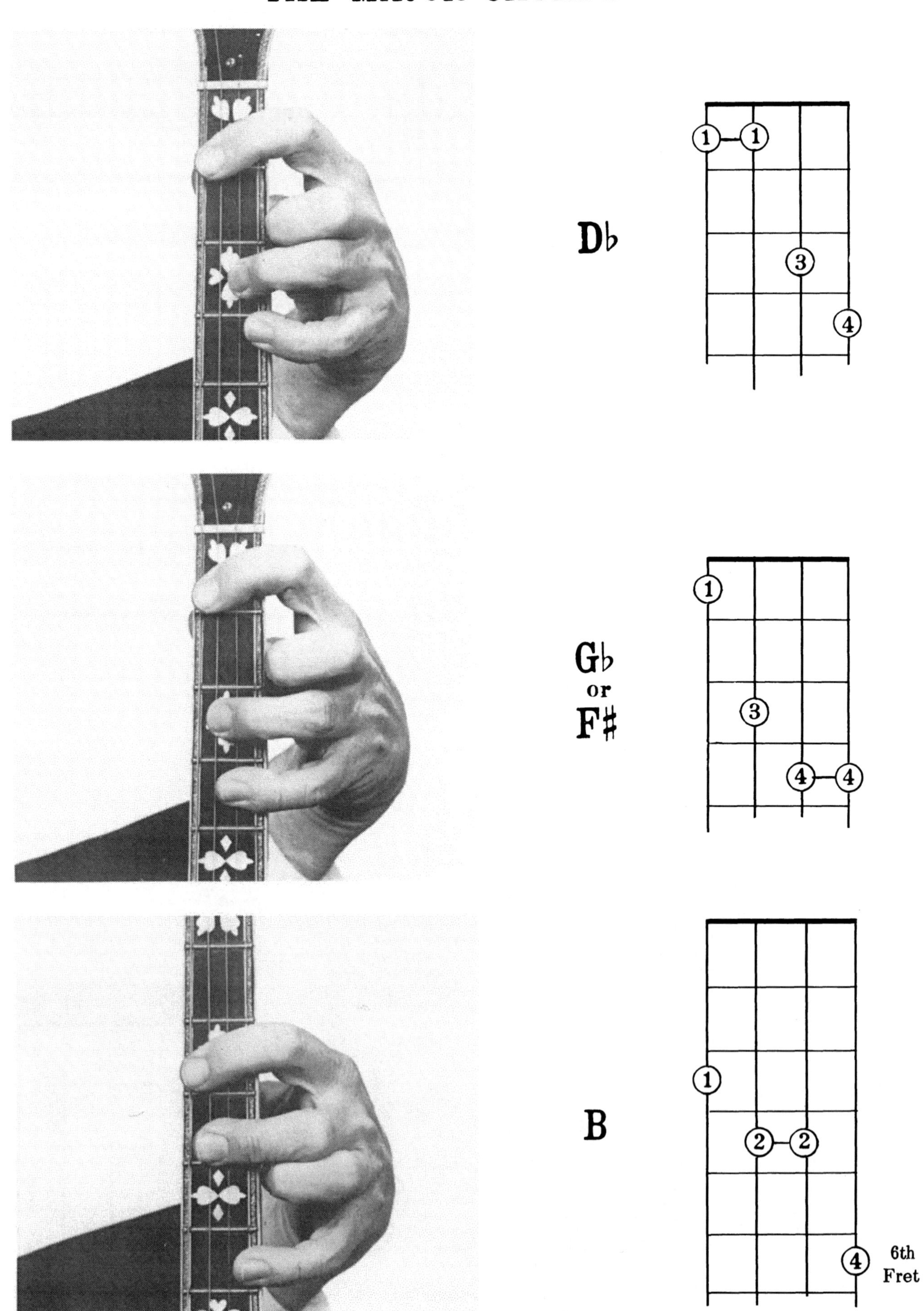

THE MINOR CHORDS
(m = Minor)

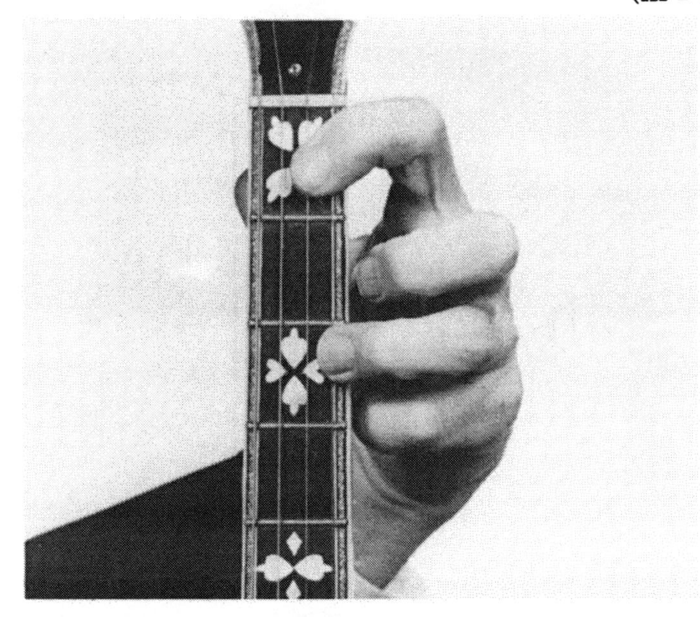

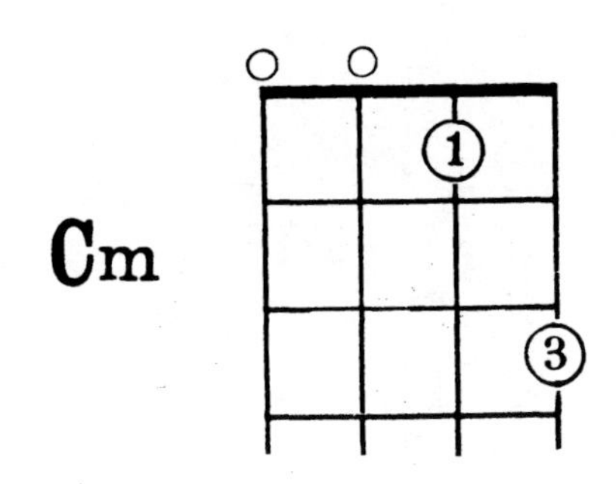

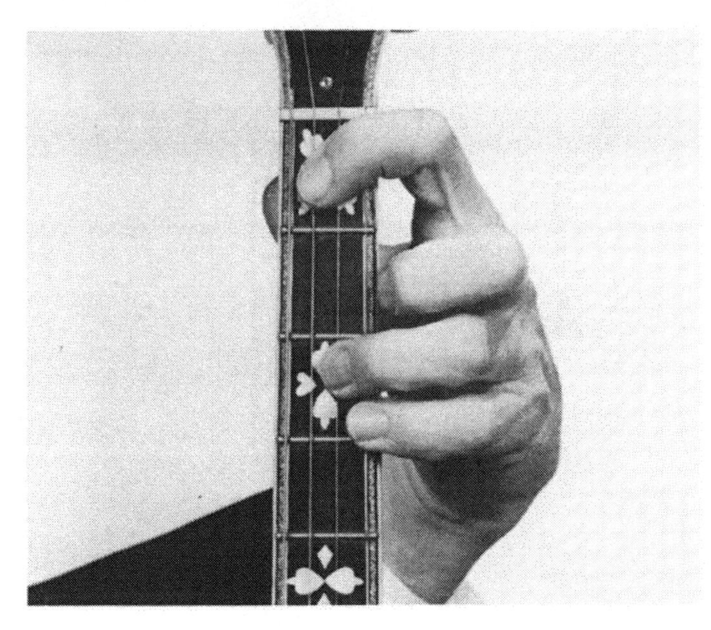

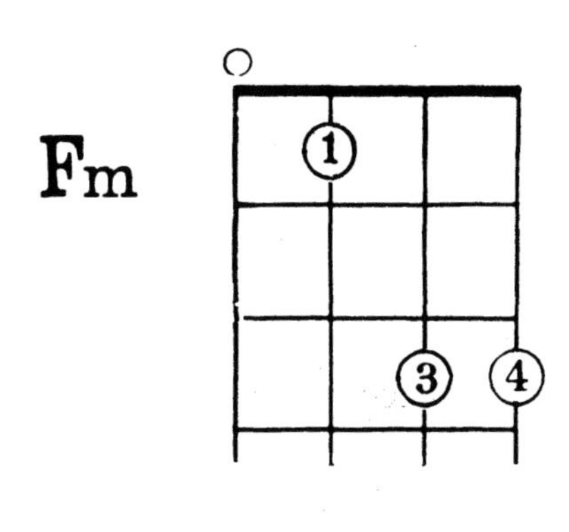

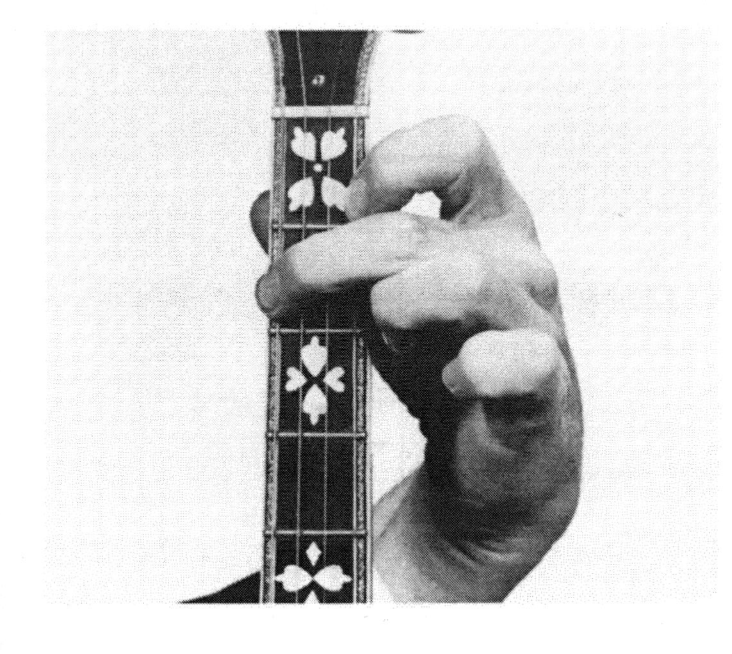

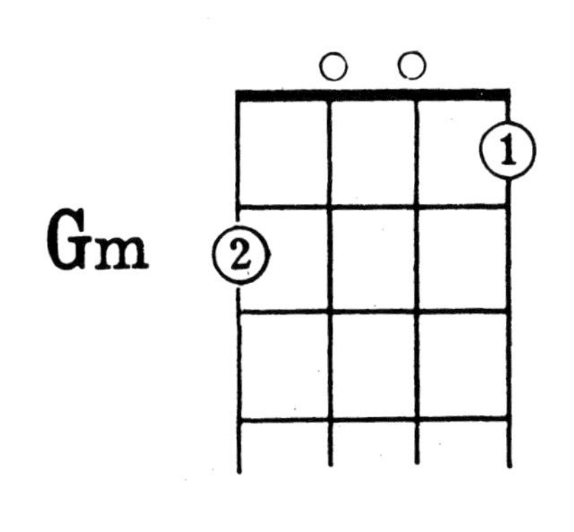

THE MINOR CHORDS

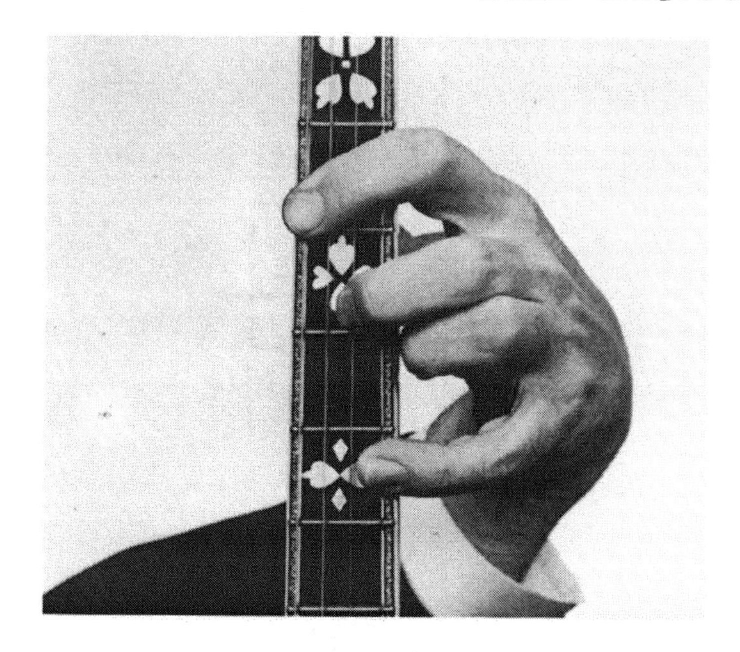

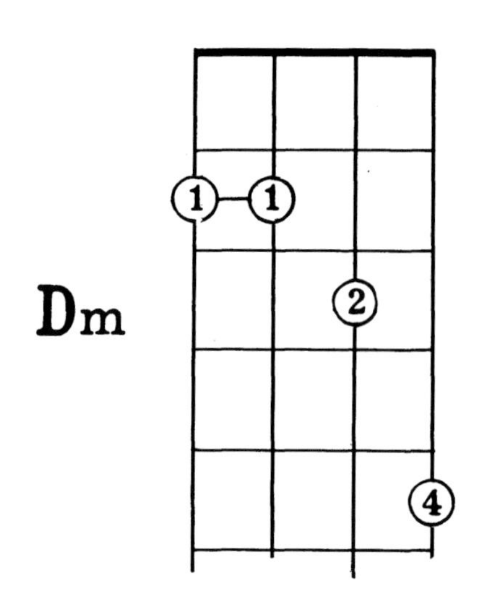

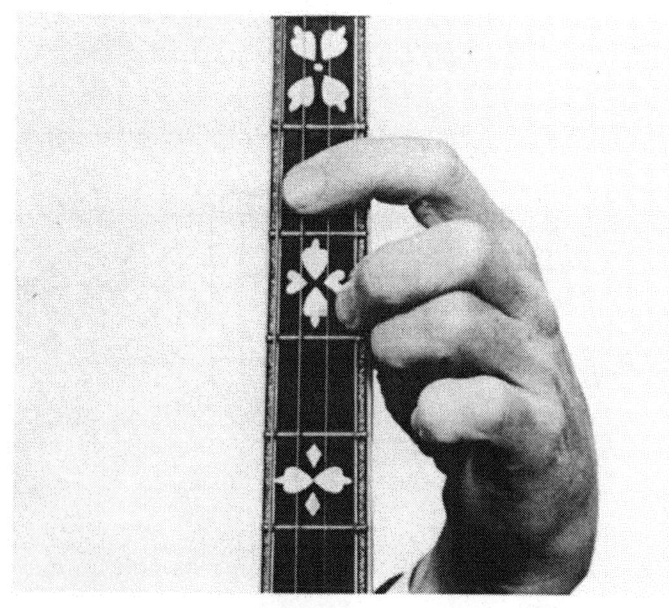

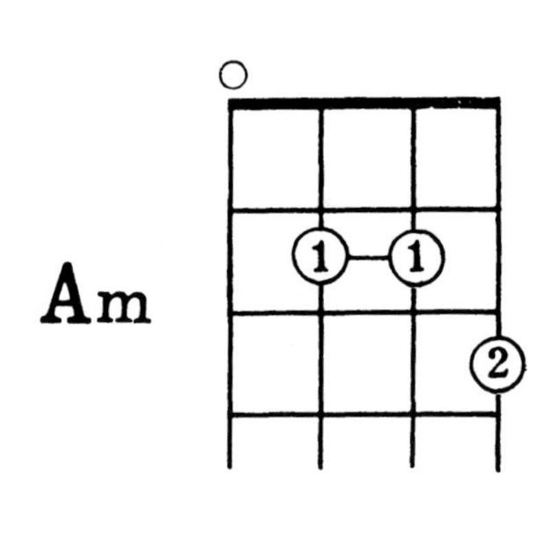

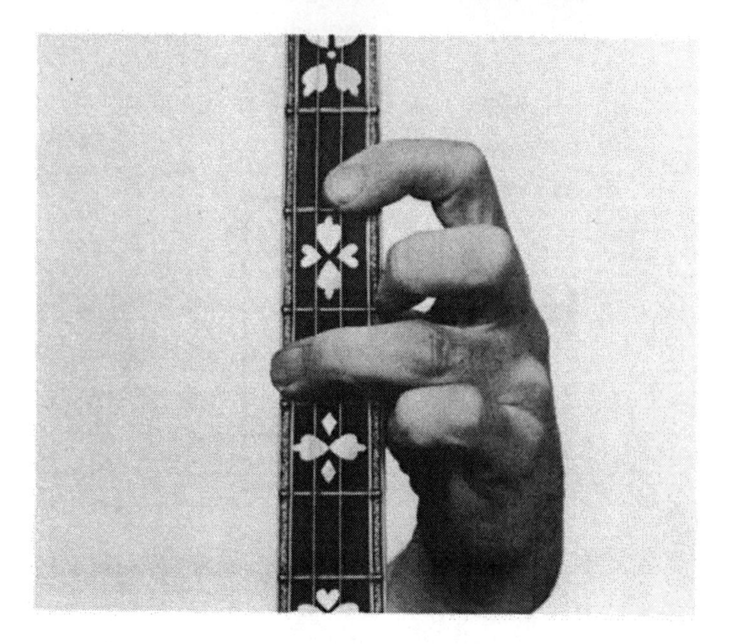

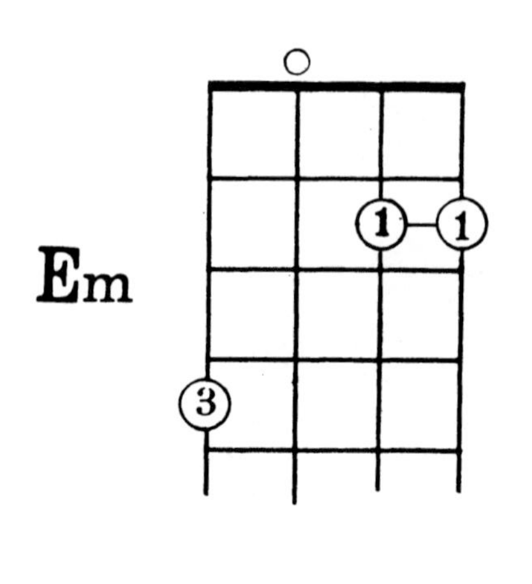

THE MINOR CHORDS

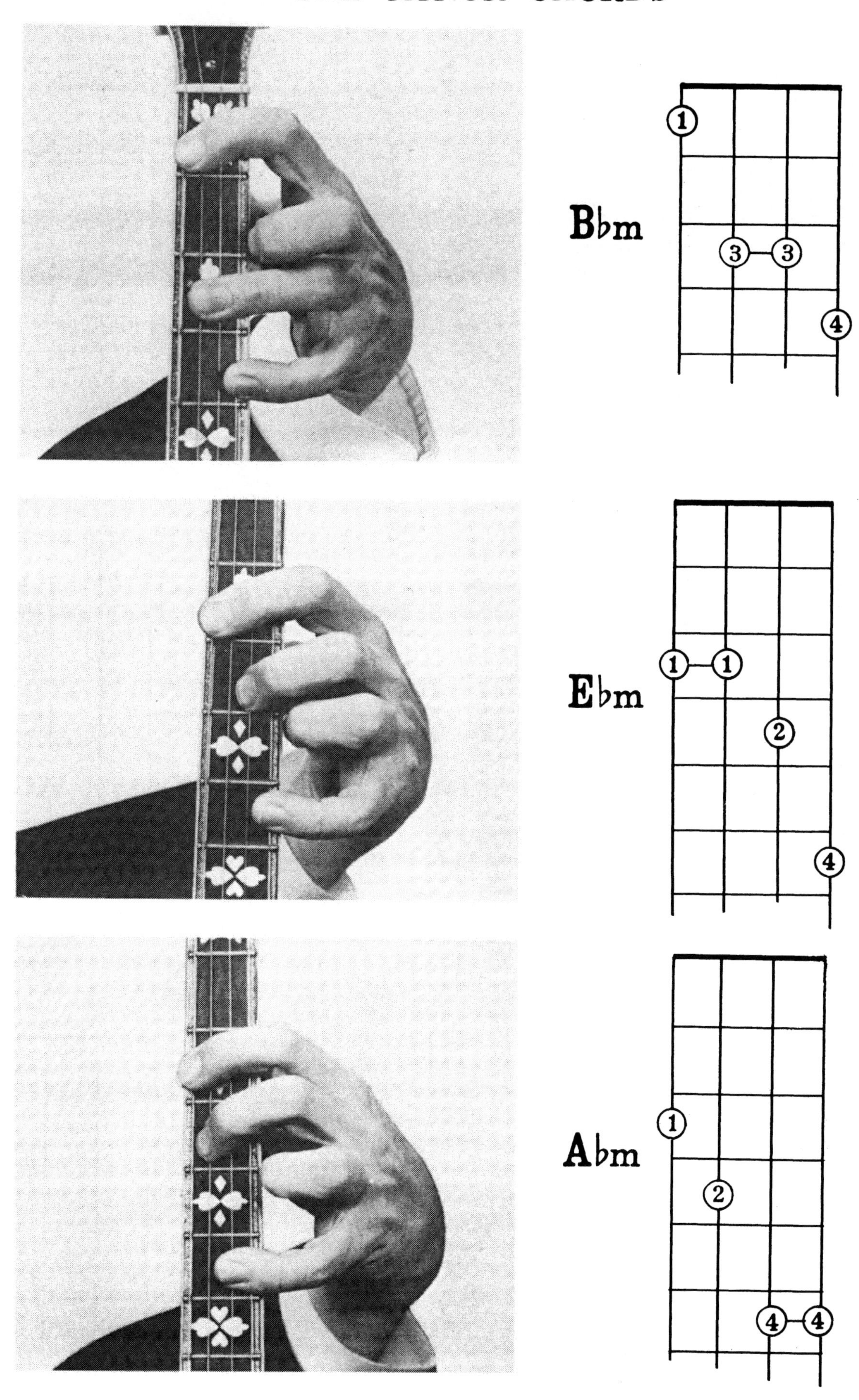

THE MINOR CHORDS

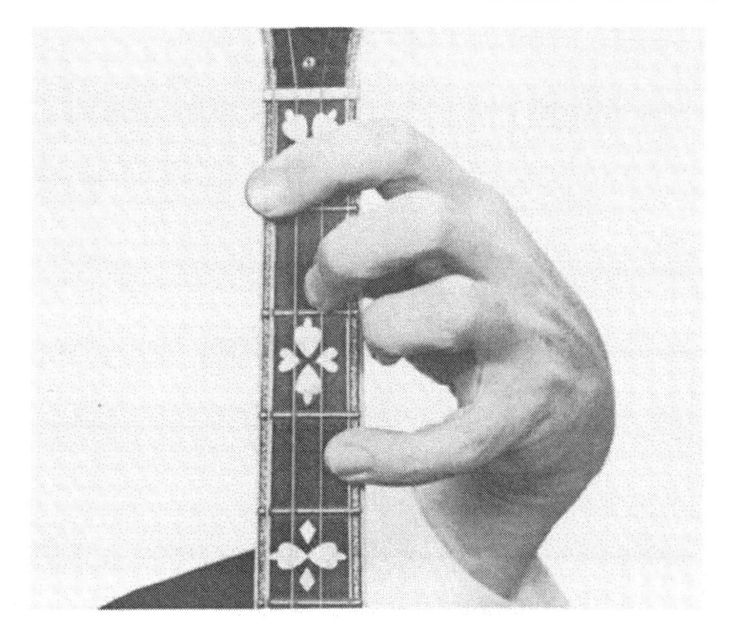

D♭m

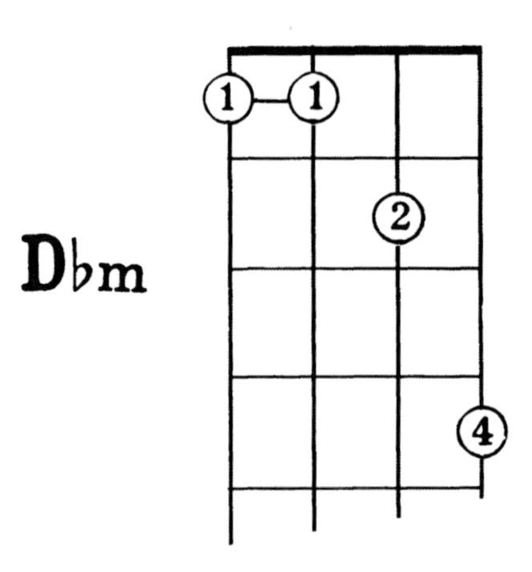

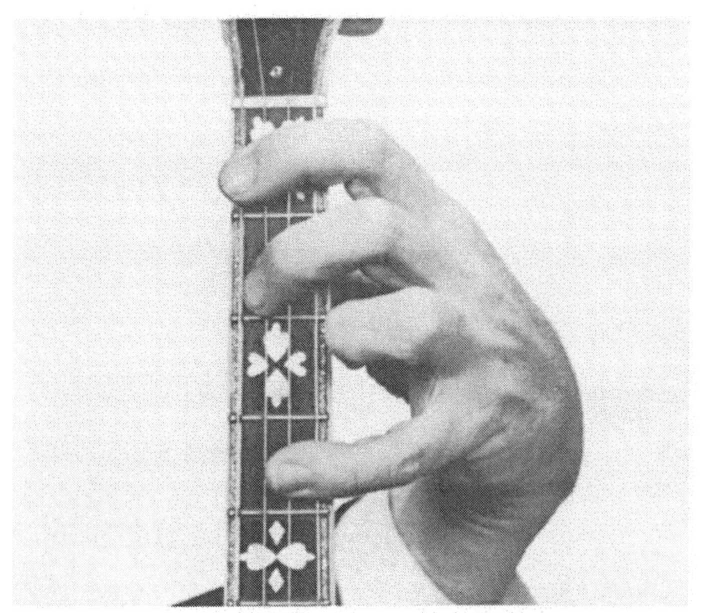

G♭m
or
F♯m

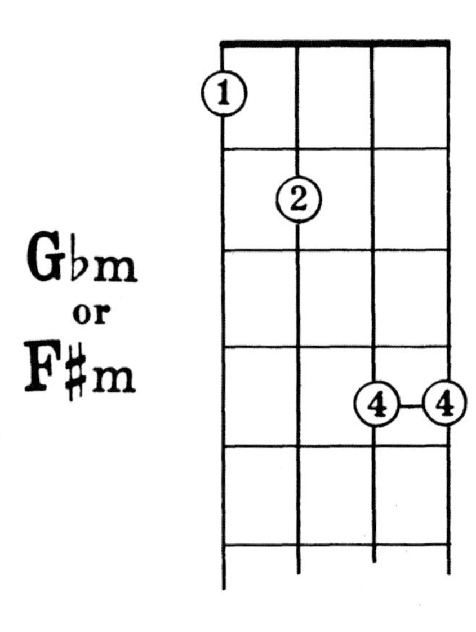

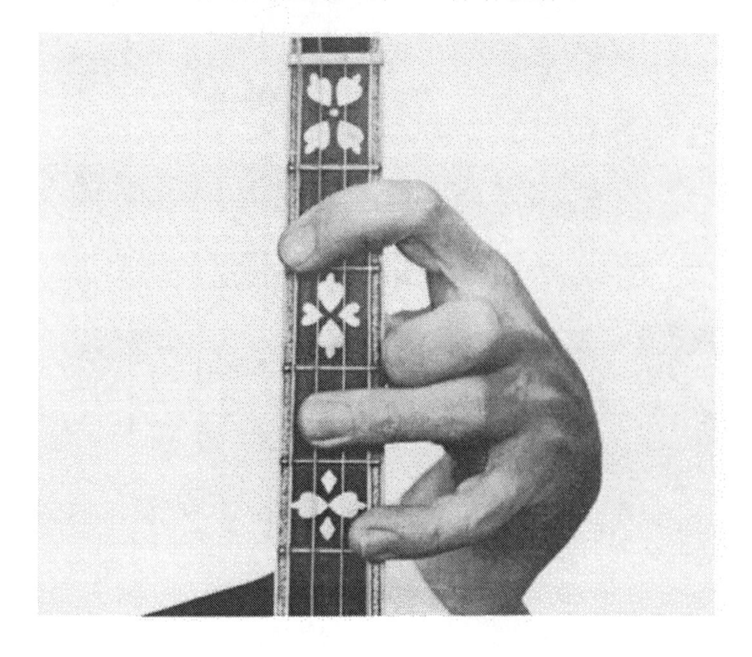

Bm

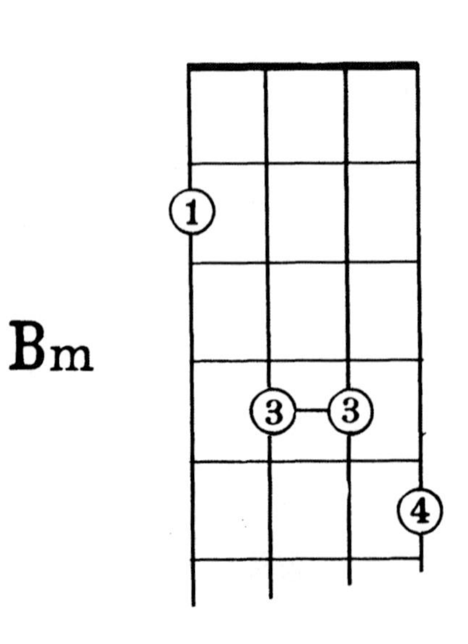

THE SEVENTH CHORDS

(7 = Seventh Chord)

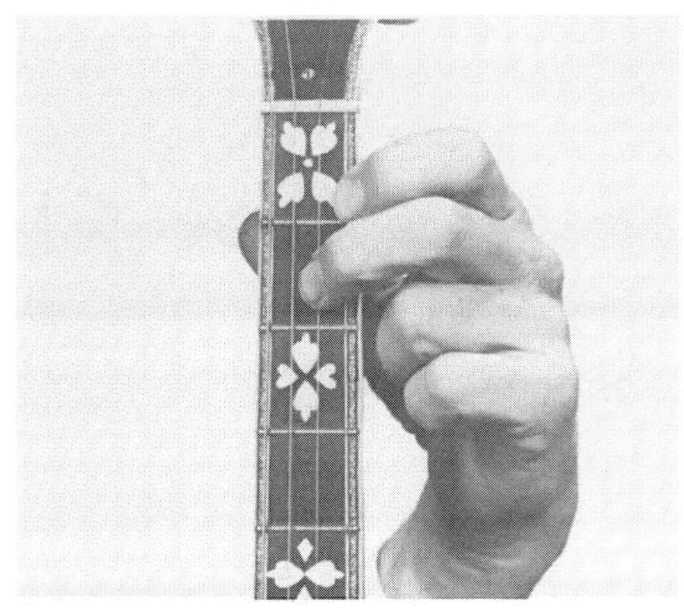

C7

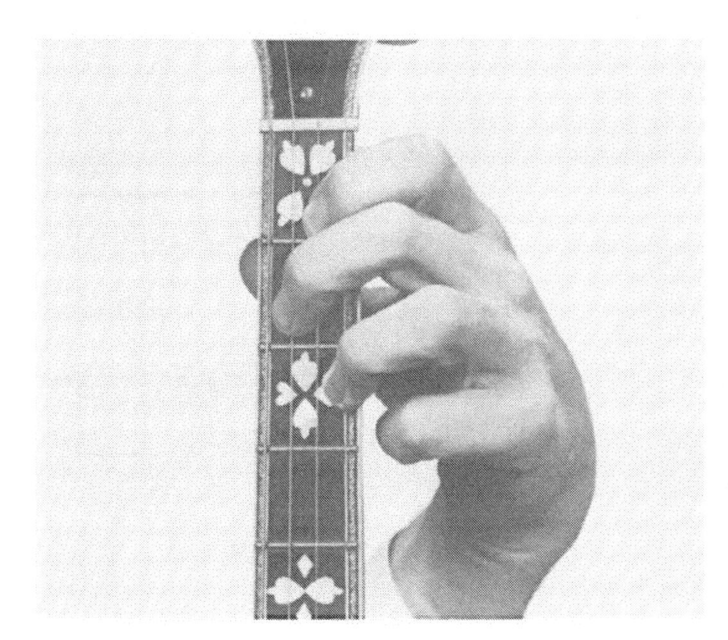

F7

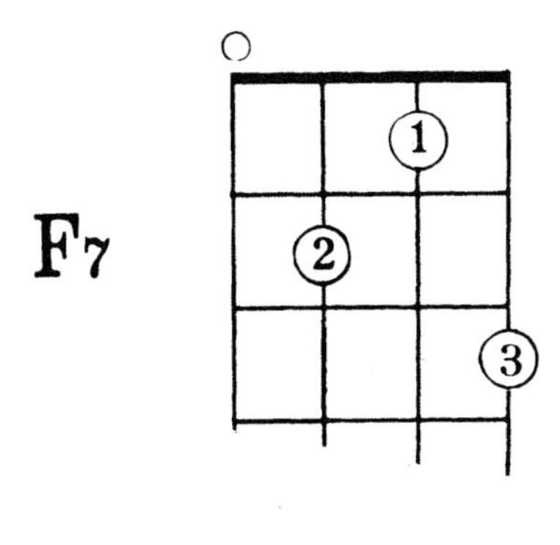

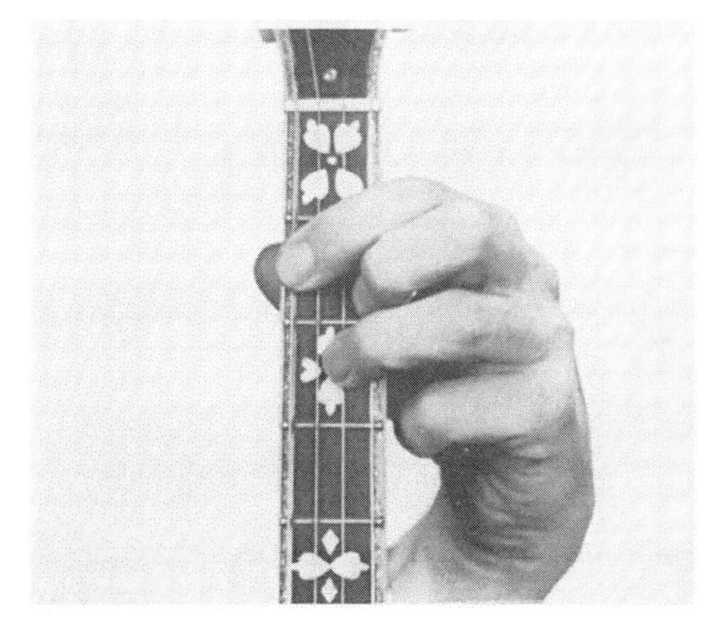

G7

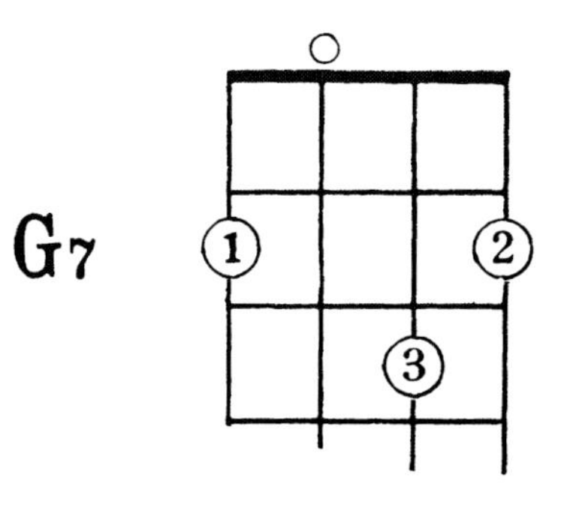

THE SEVENTH CHORDS

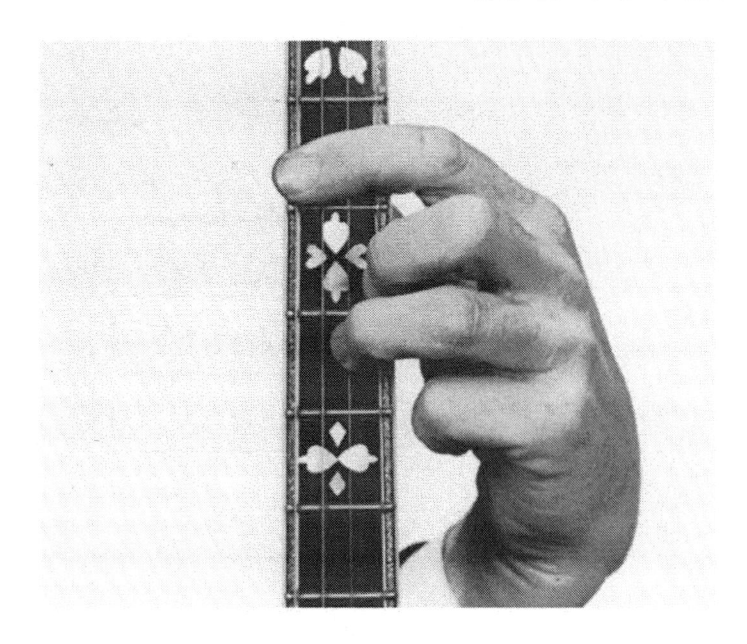

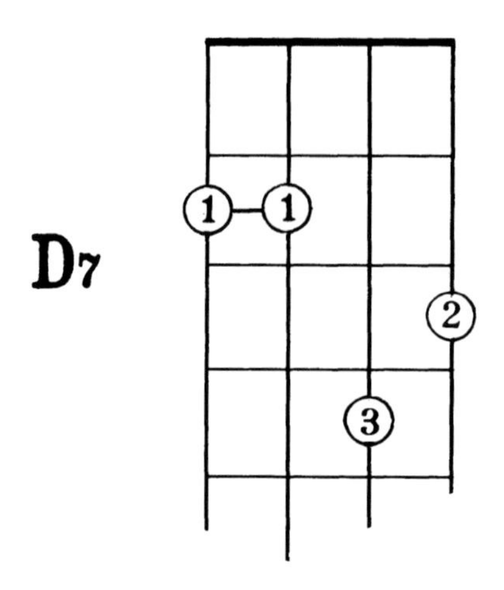

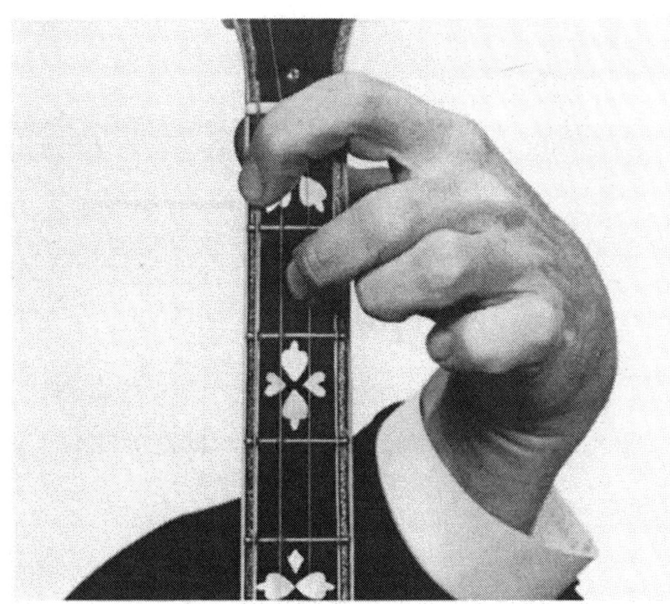

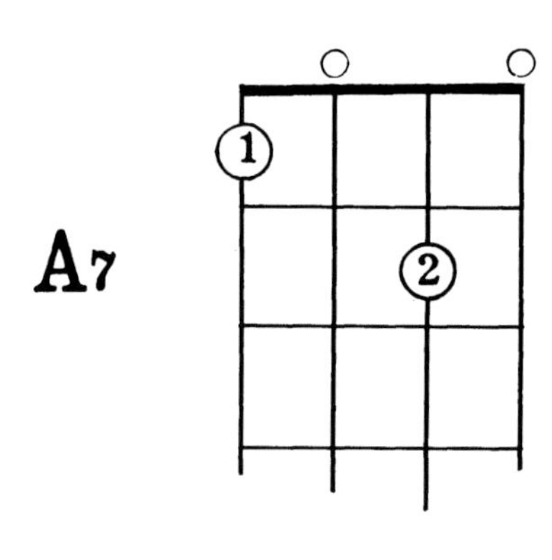

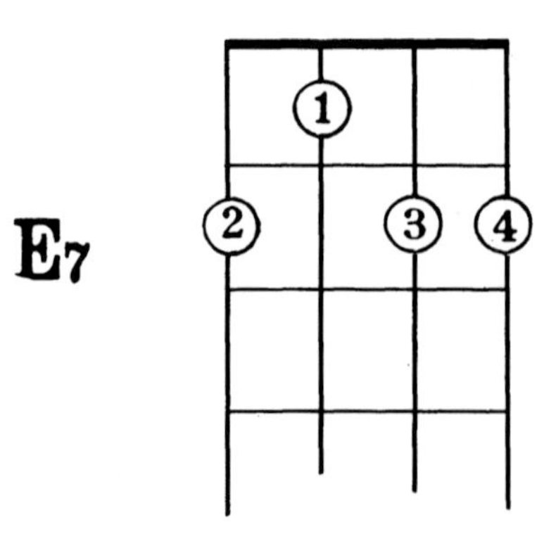

THE SEVENTH CHORDS

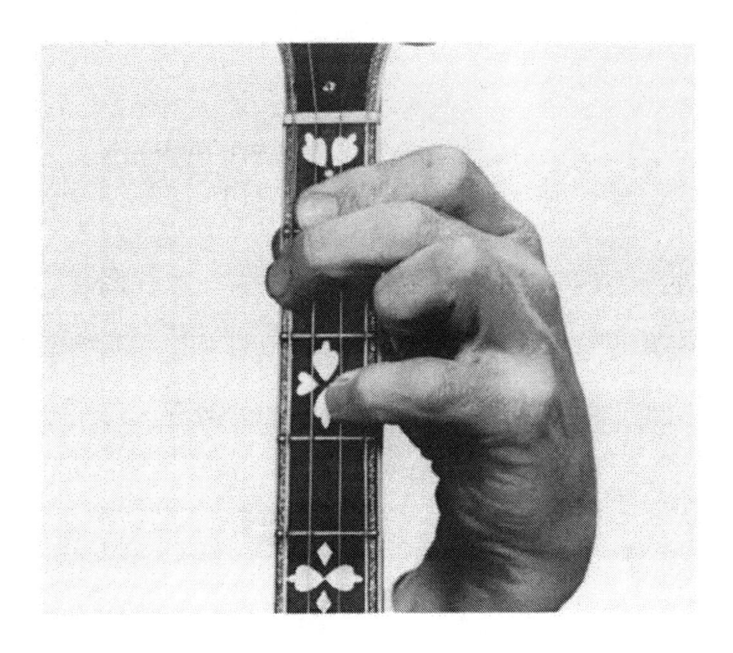

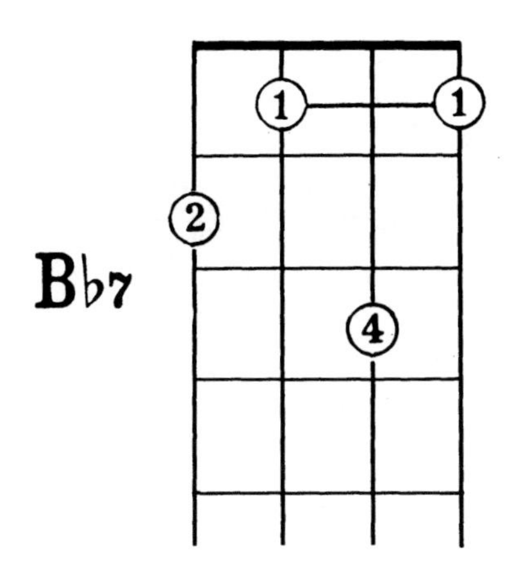

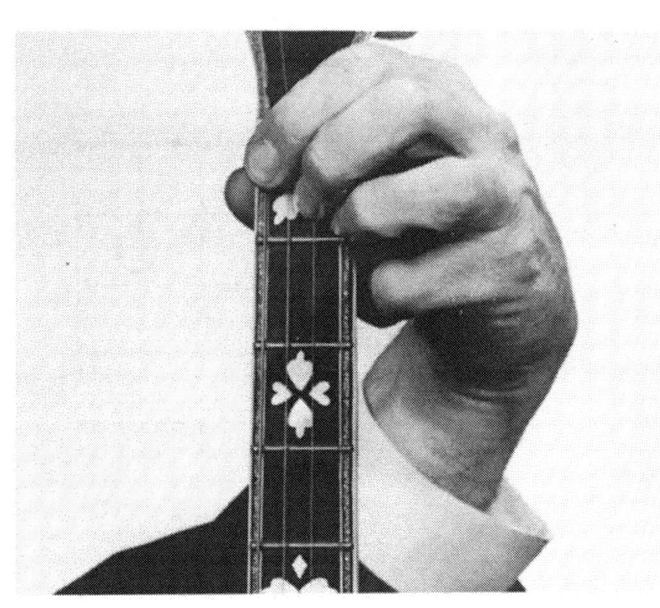

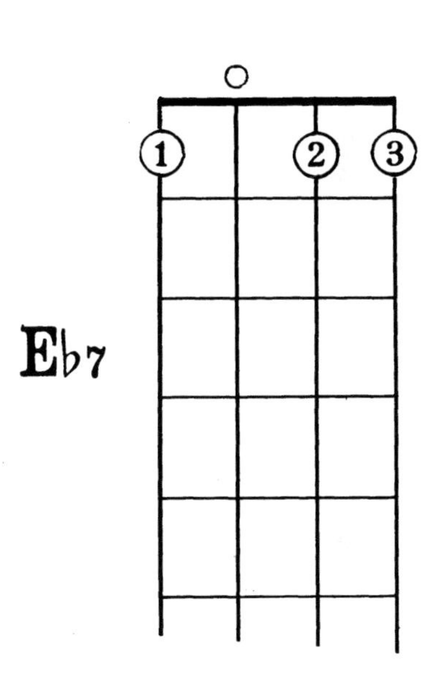

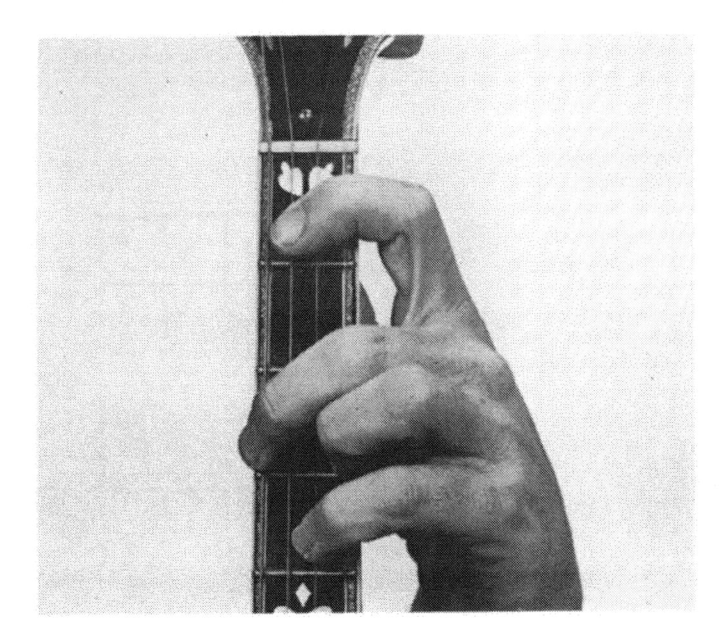

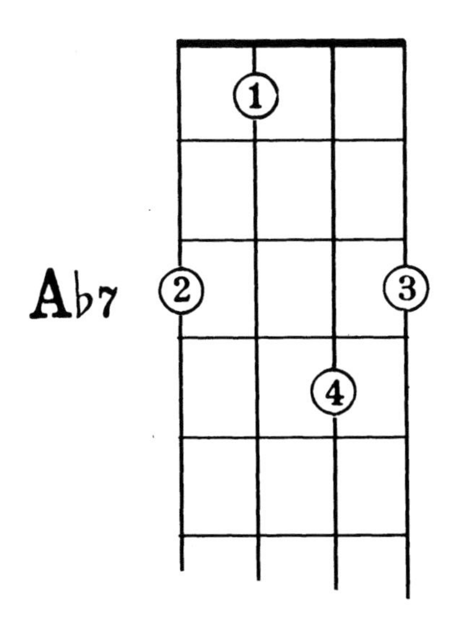

THE SEVENTH CHORDS

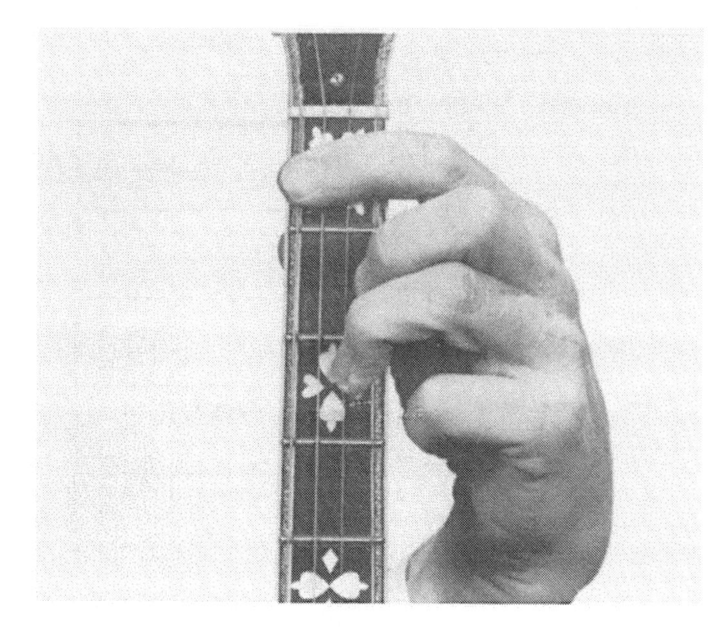

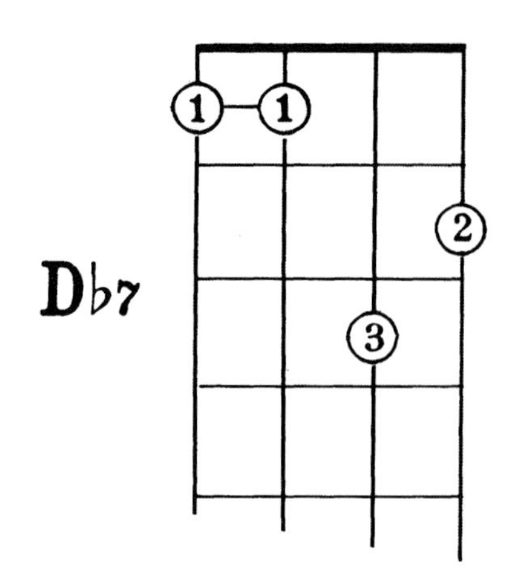

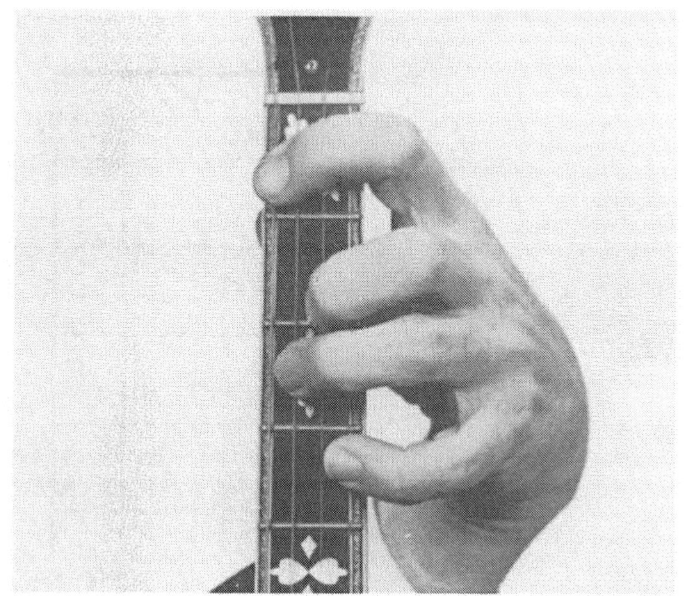

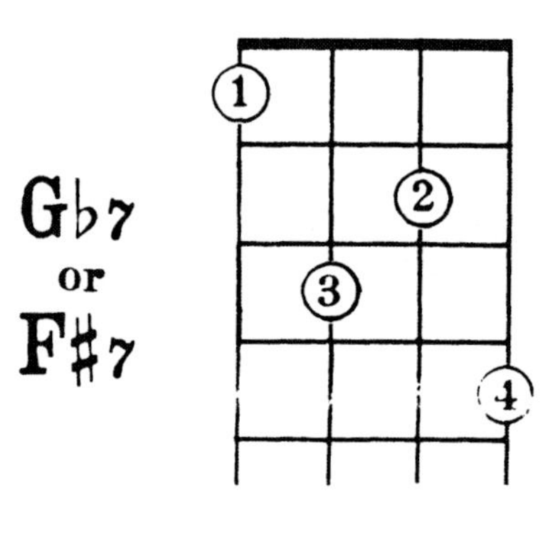

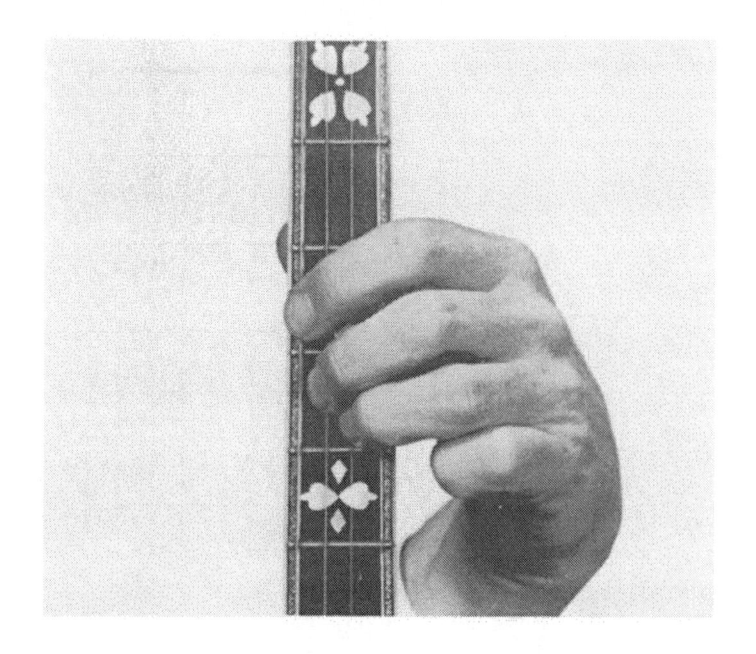

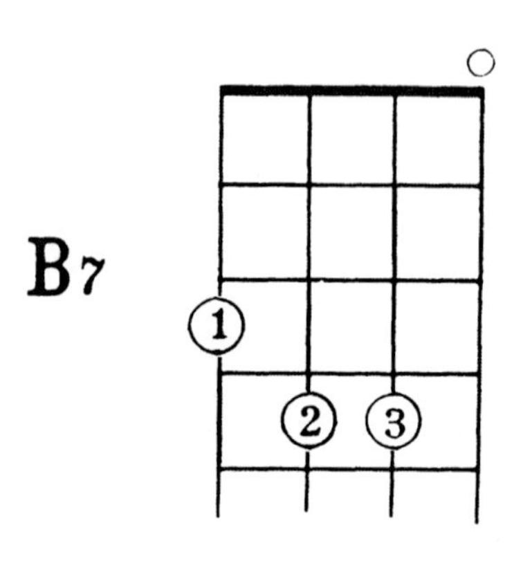

THE DIMINISHED CHORDS

(–) = Diminished)

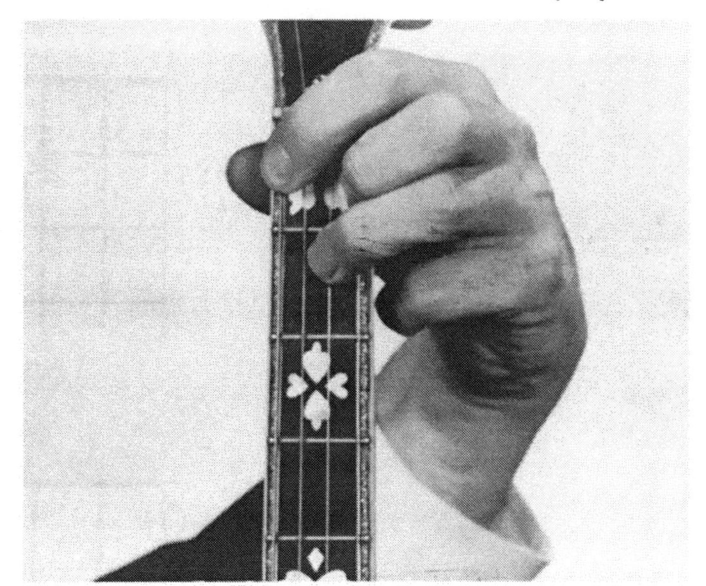

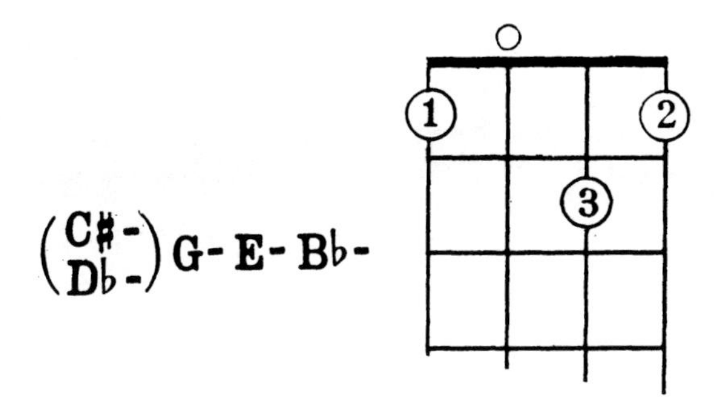

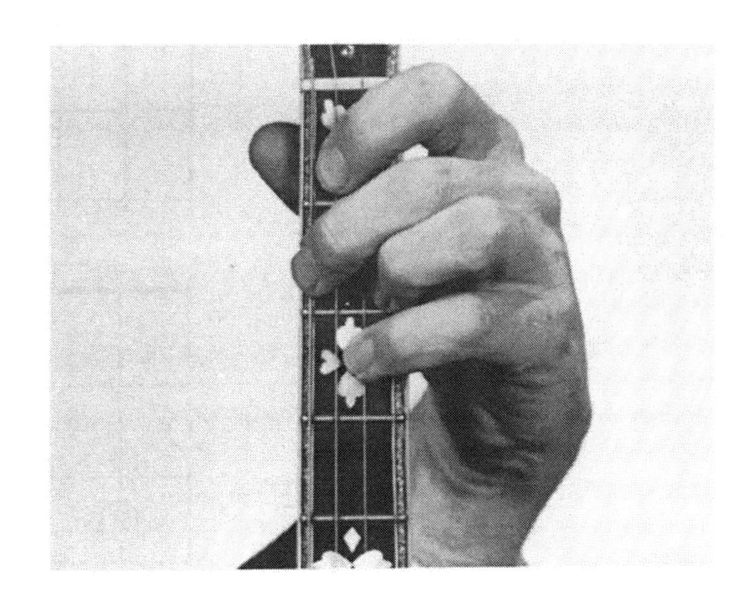

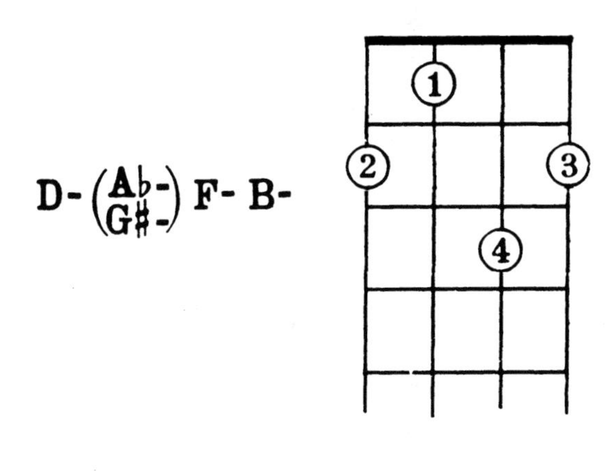

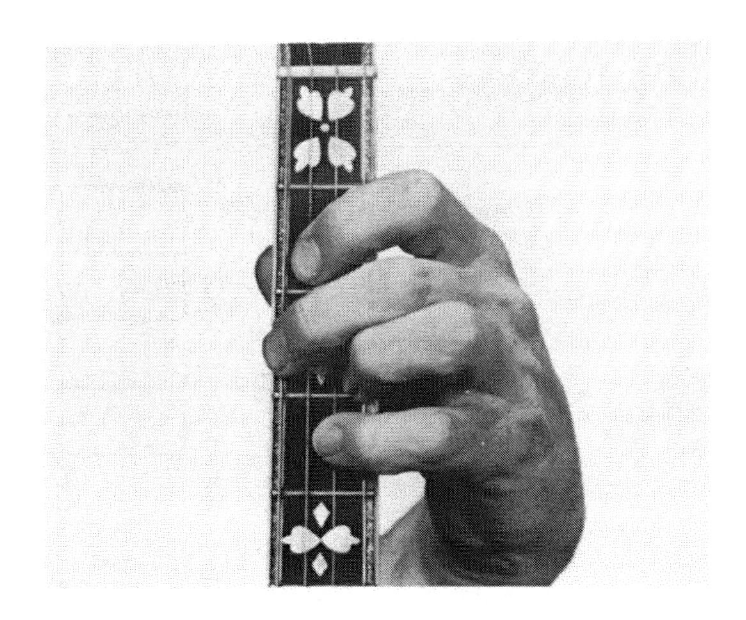

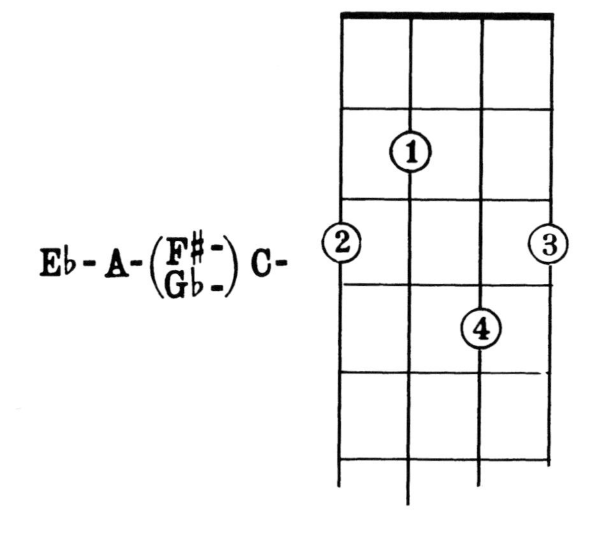

Each Diminished form can represent four different chords.

THE AUGMENTED CHORDS

(+) = Augmented

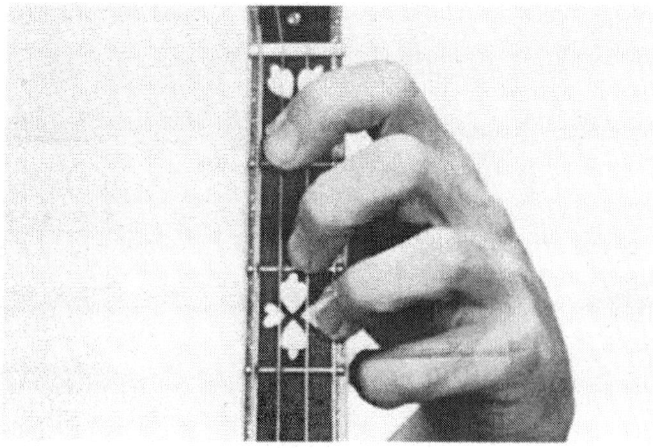

C+ E+ (G♯+ / A♭+)

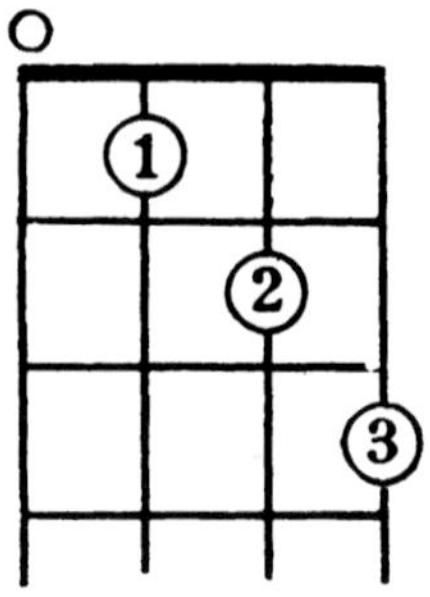

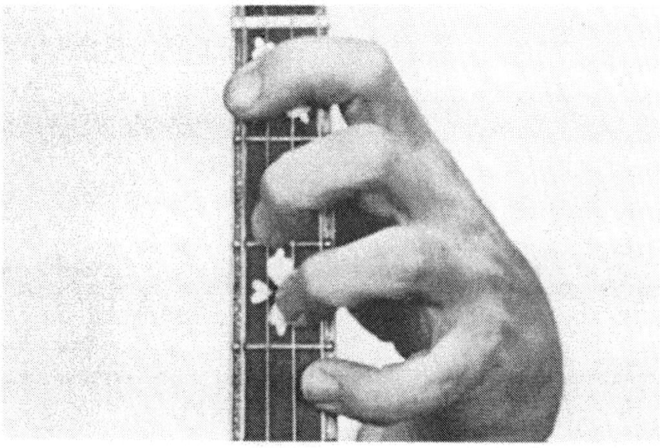

(C♯+ / D♭+) A+ F+

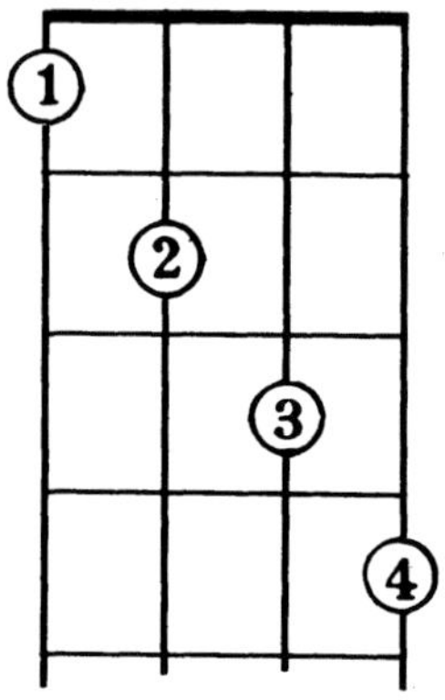

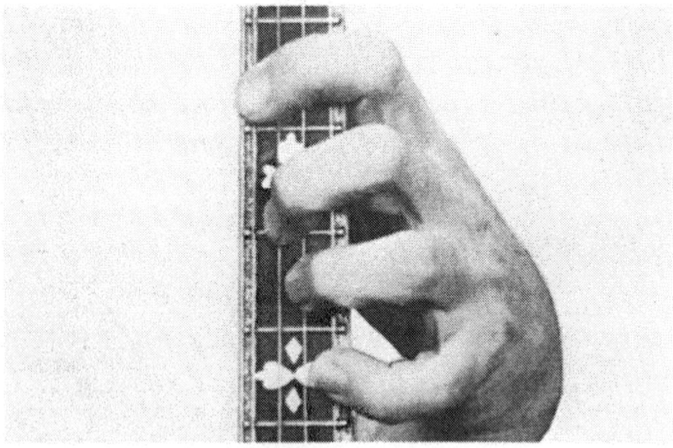

D+ (F♯+ / G♭+) B♭+

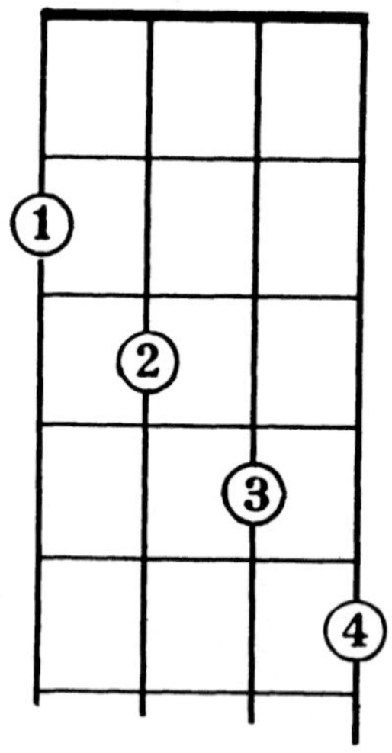

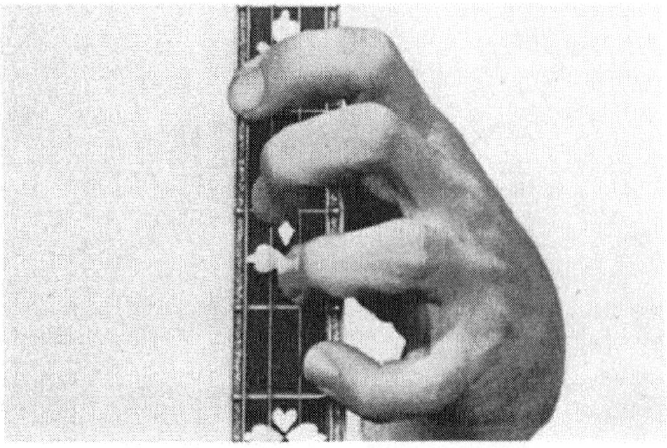

E♭+ G+ B+

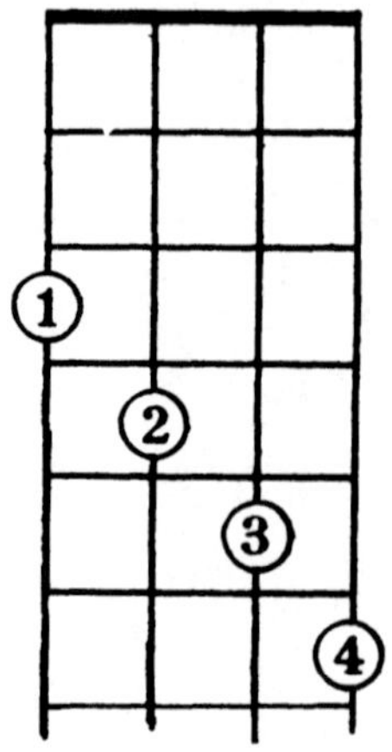

Each form represents three chords.

THE NINTH CHORDS

(9 = Ninth)

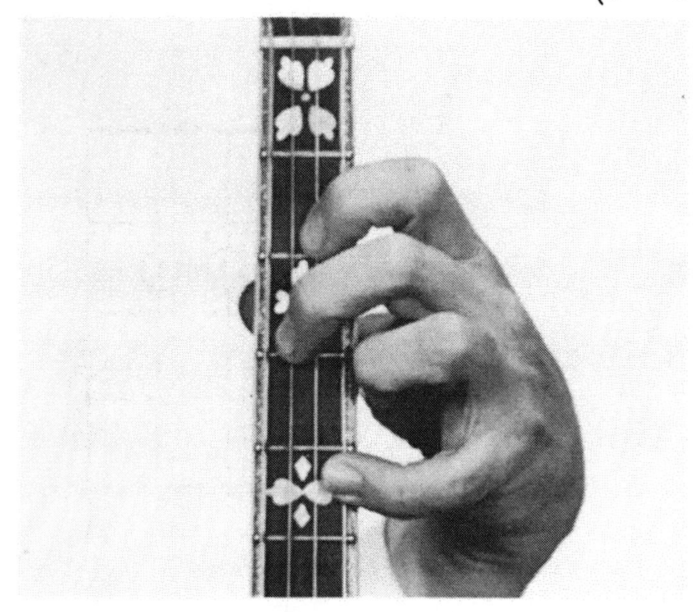

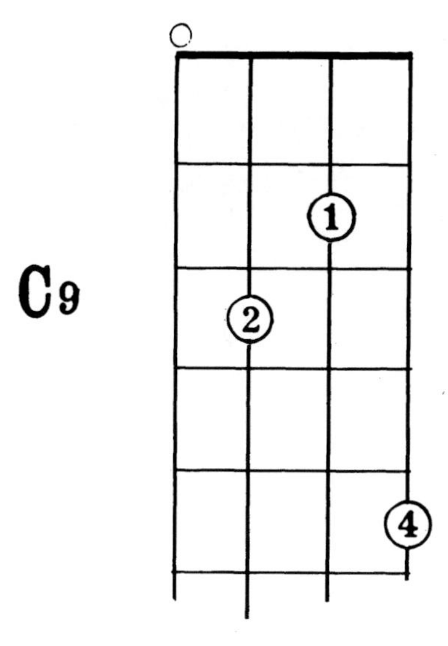

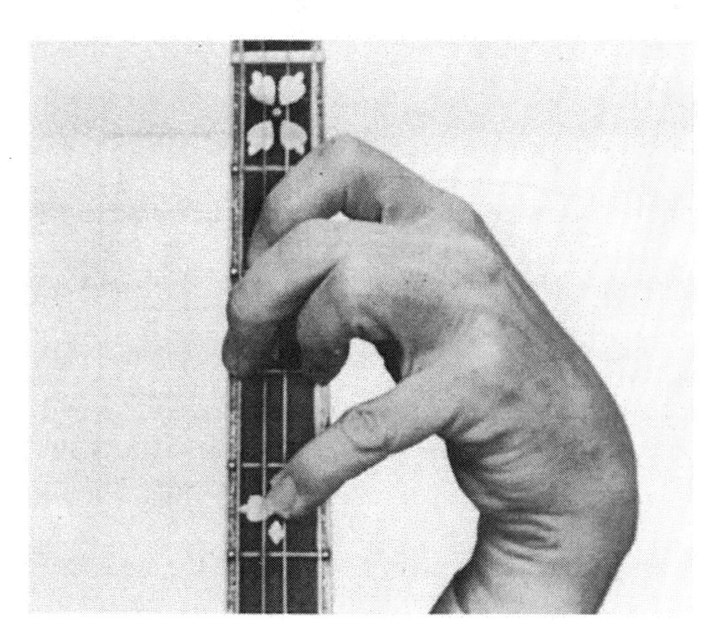

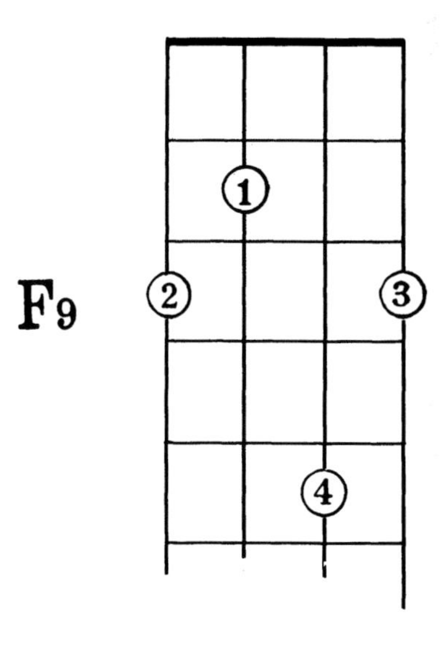

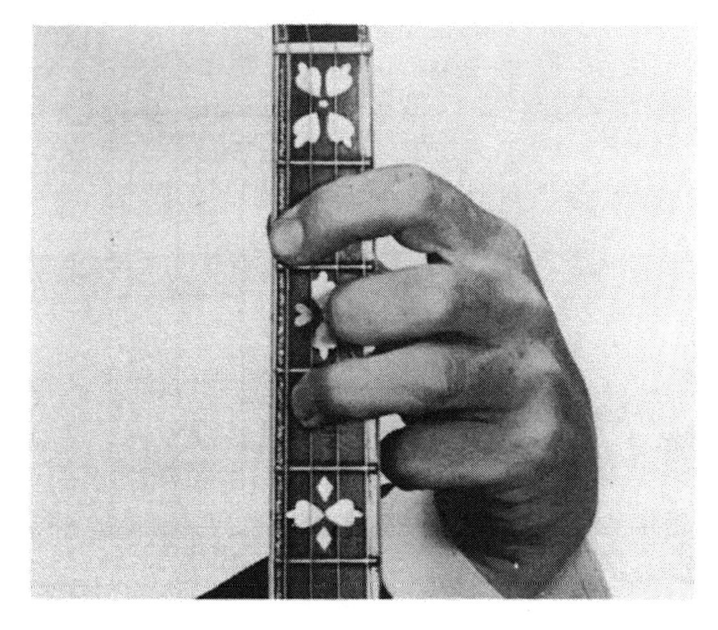

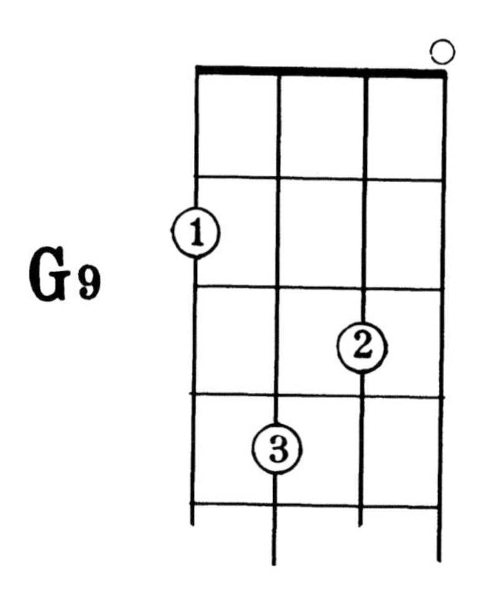

THE NINTH CHORDS

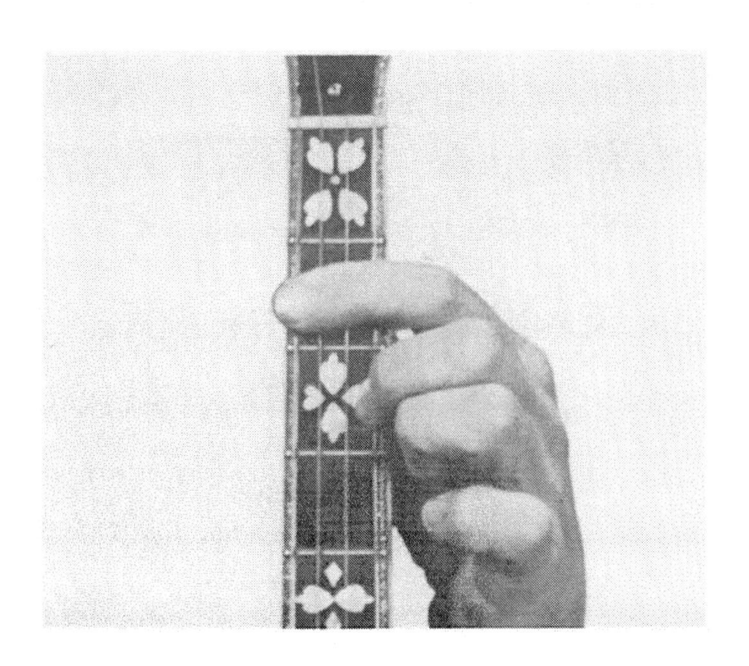

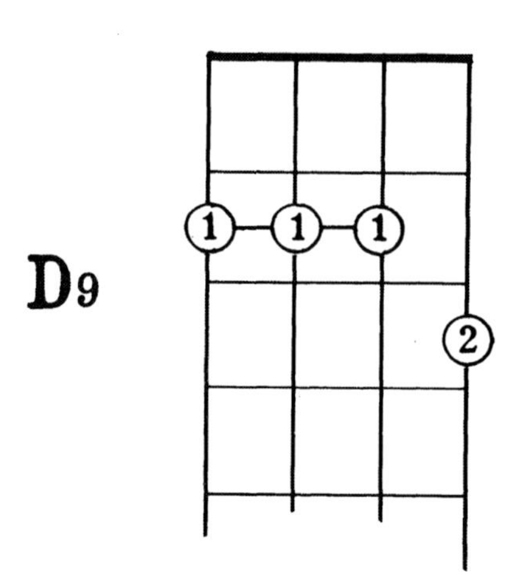

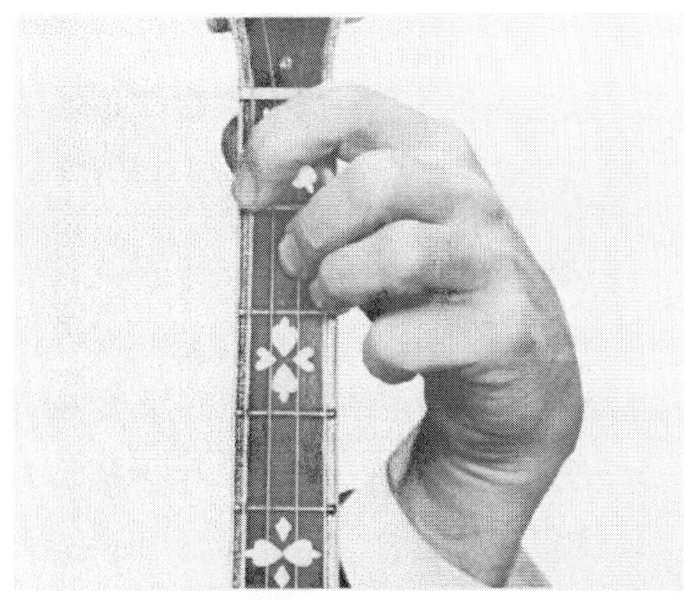

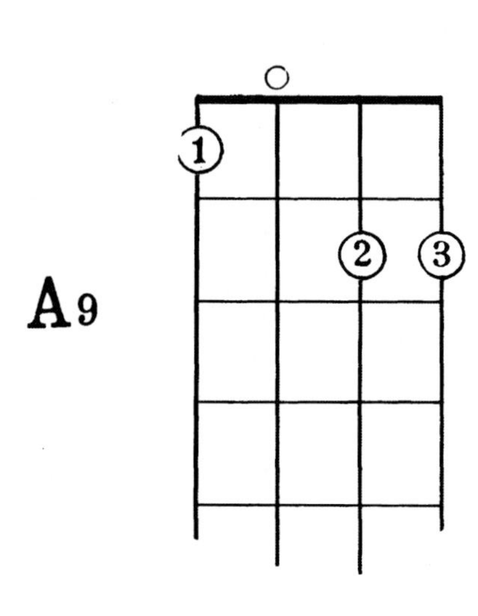

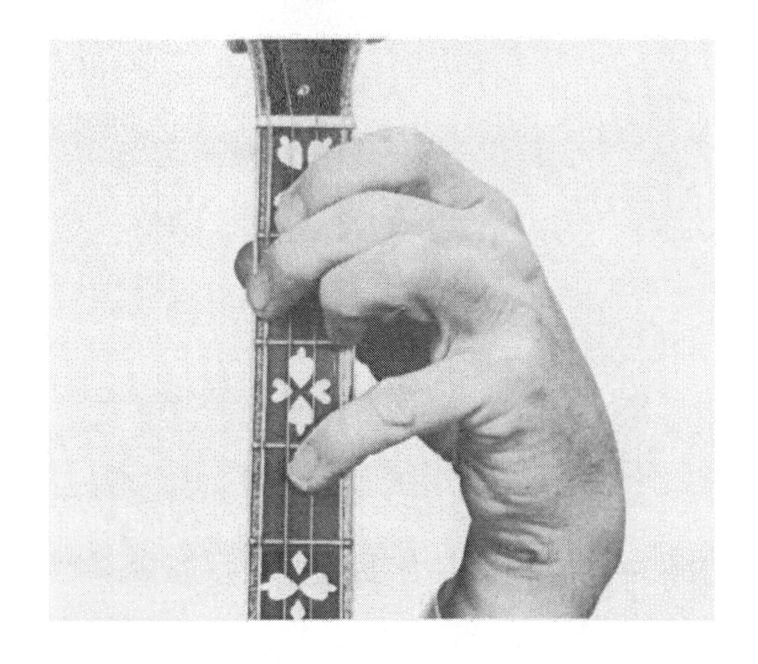

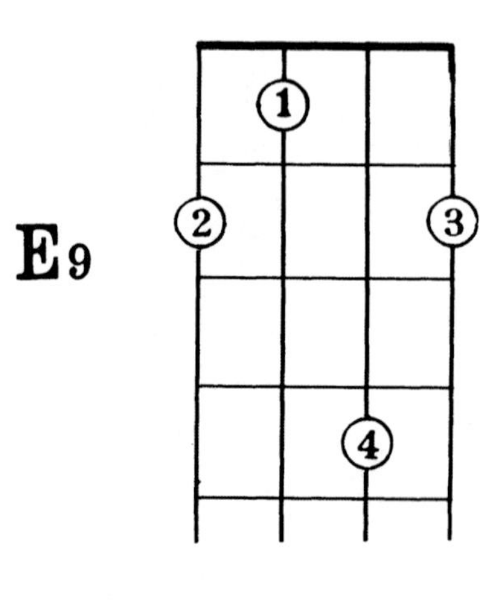

THE NINTH CHORDS

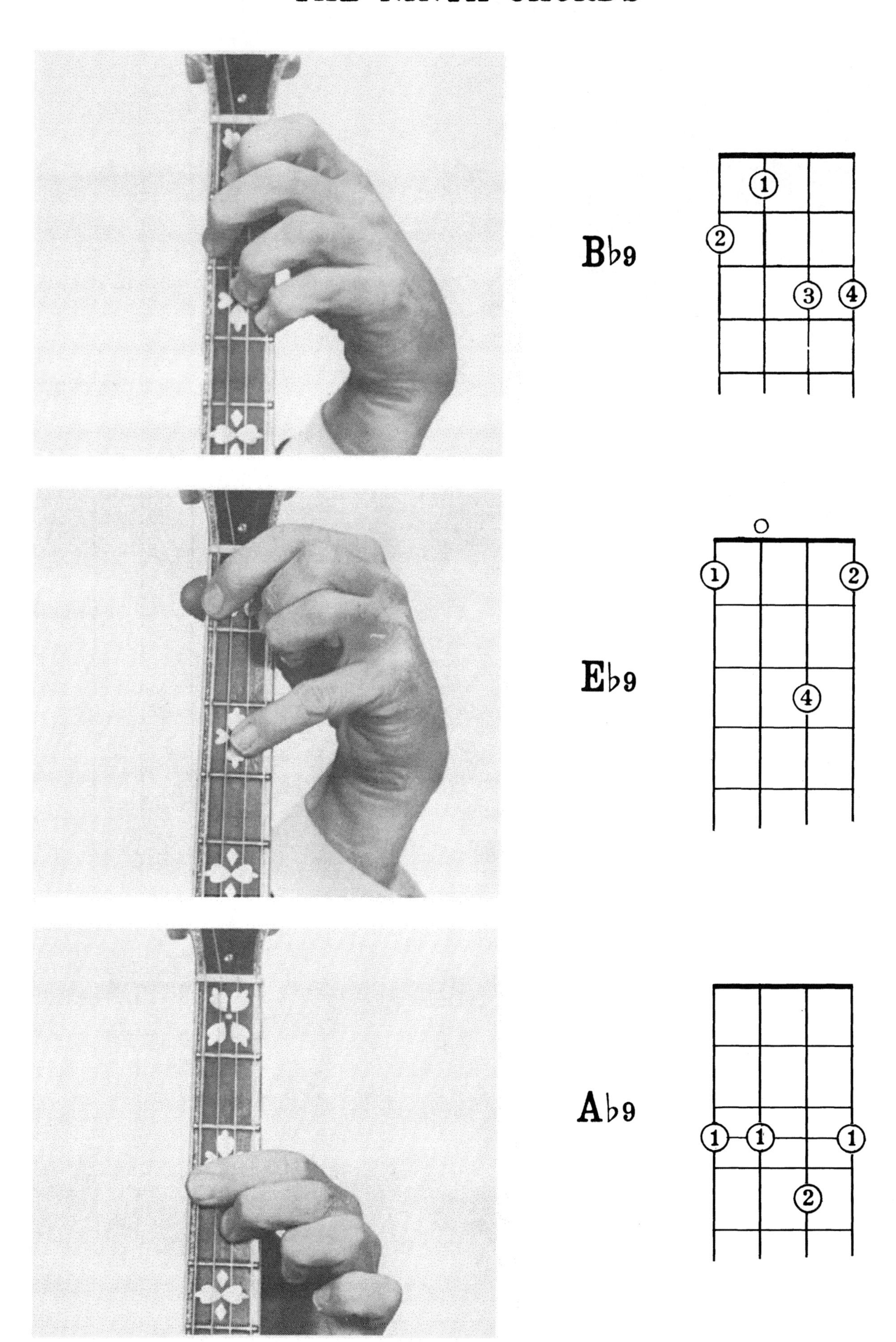

THE NINTH CHORDS

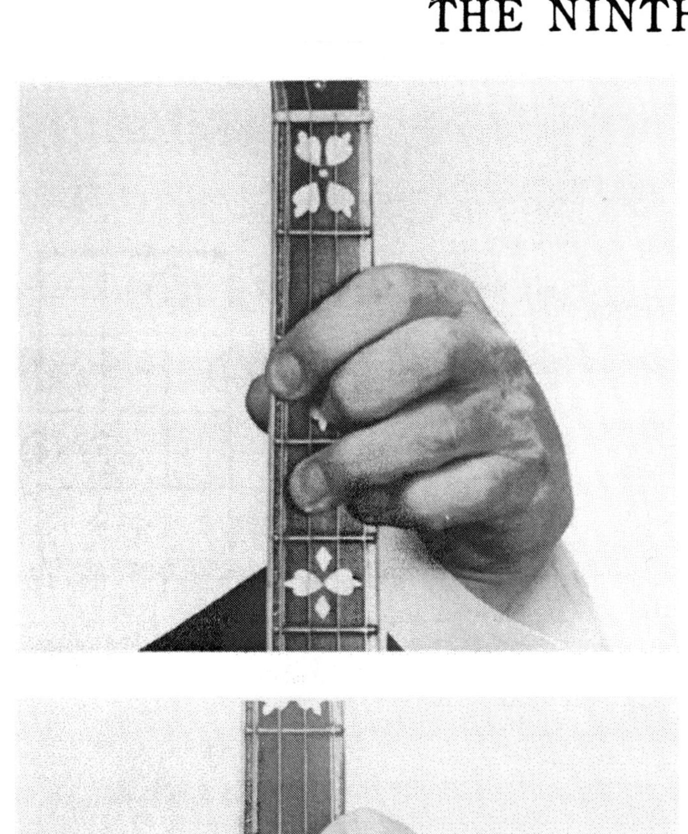

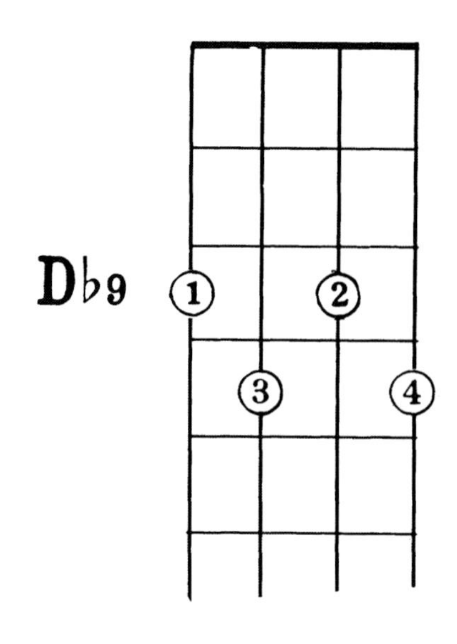

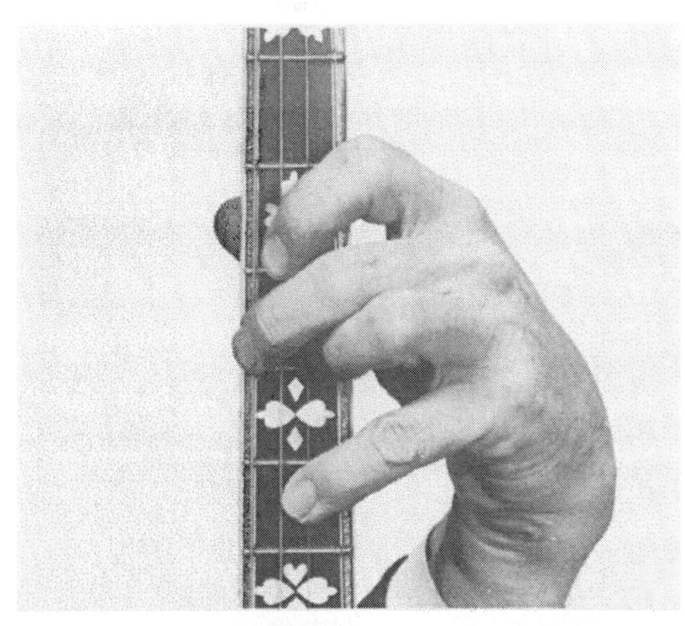

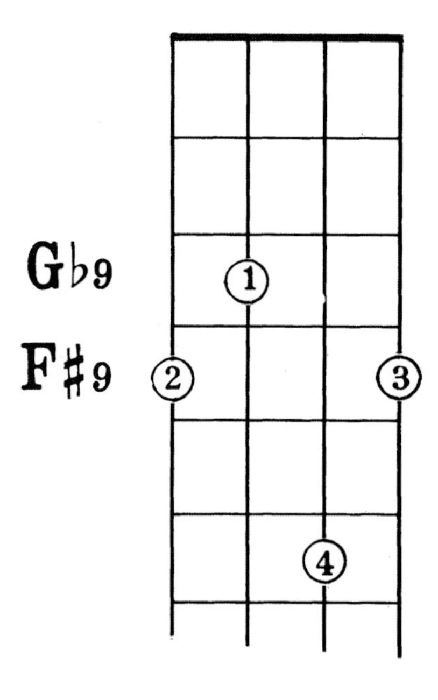

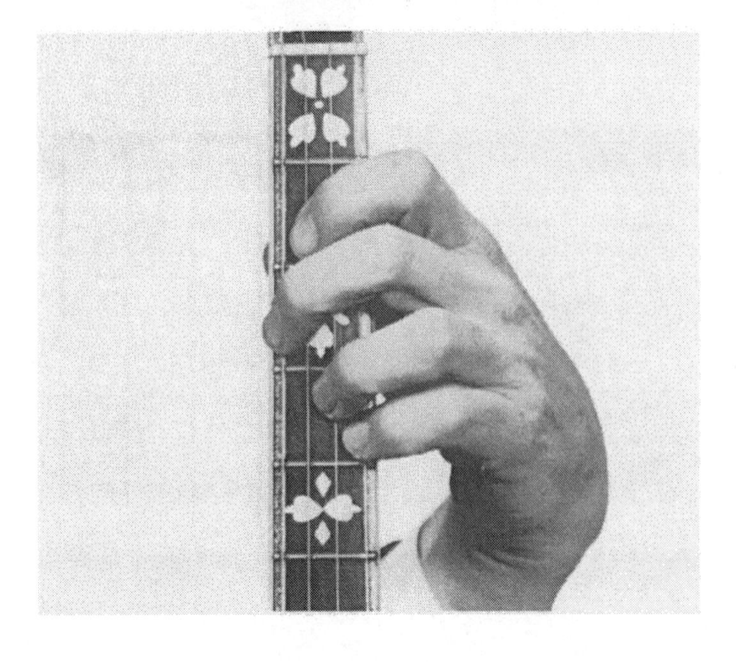

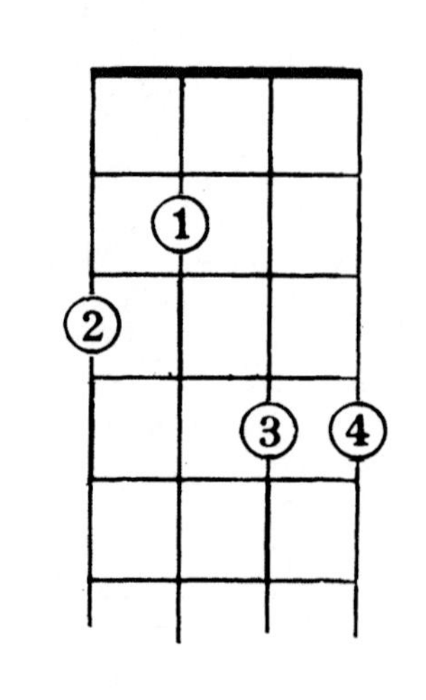

THE MAJOR SEVENTH CHORDS

(ma7 = Major Seventh)

Gma7

Cma7

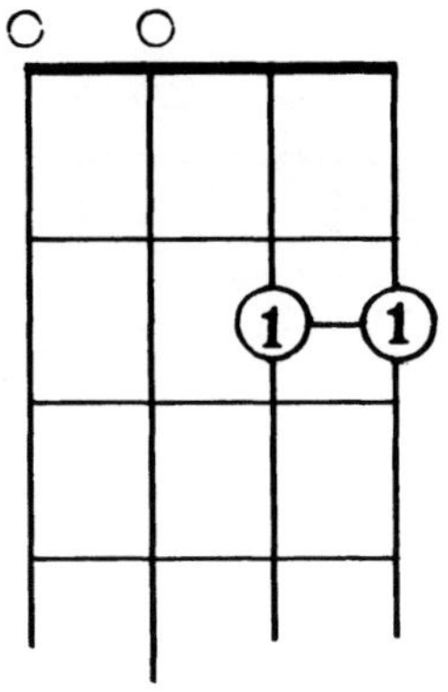

Fma7

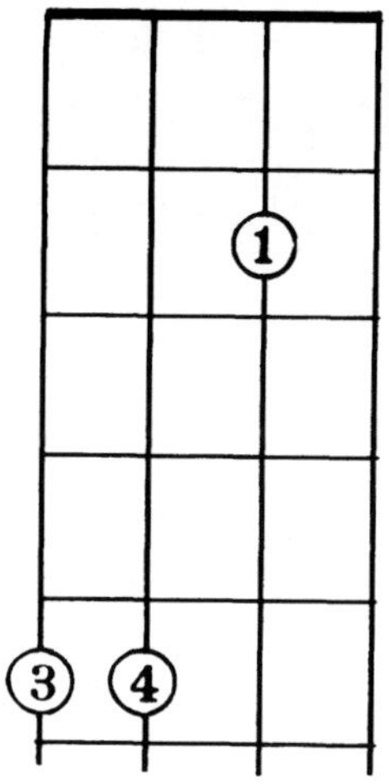

Ema7

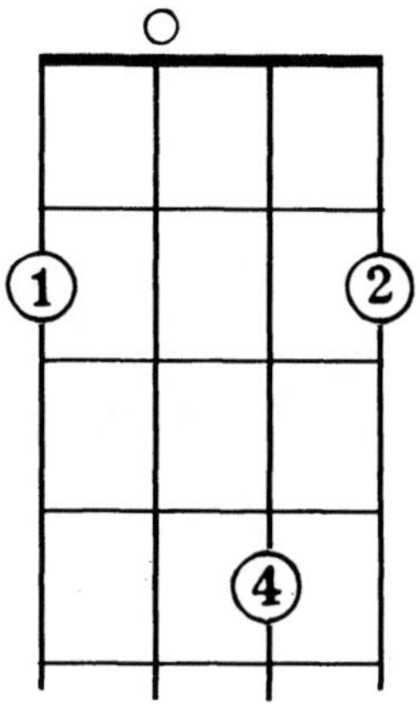

Dma7

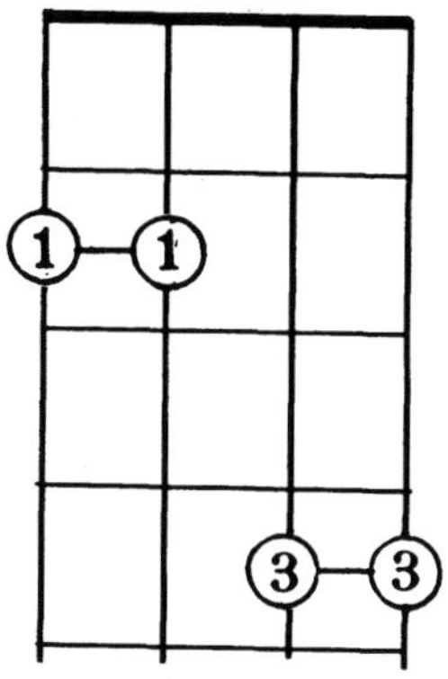

Ama7

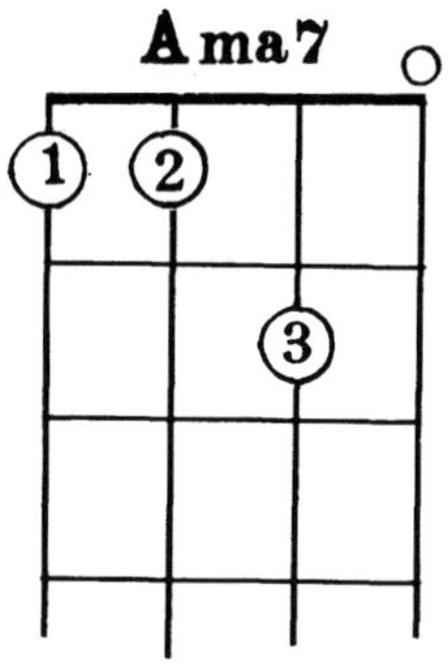

6th Fret

A♭ma7

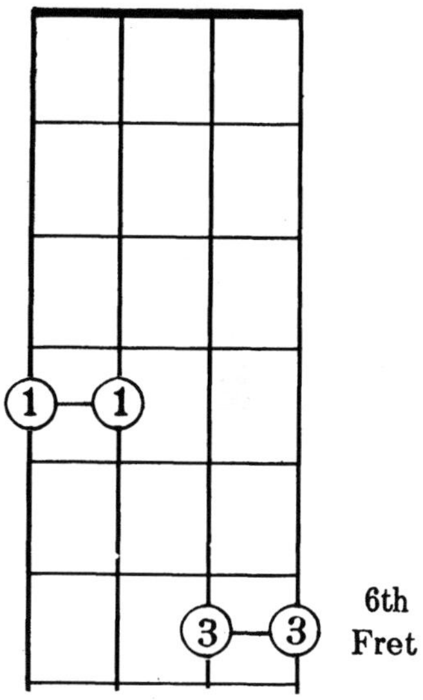

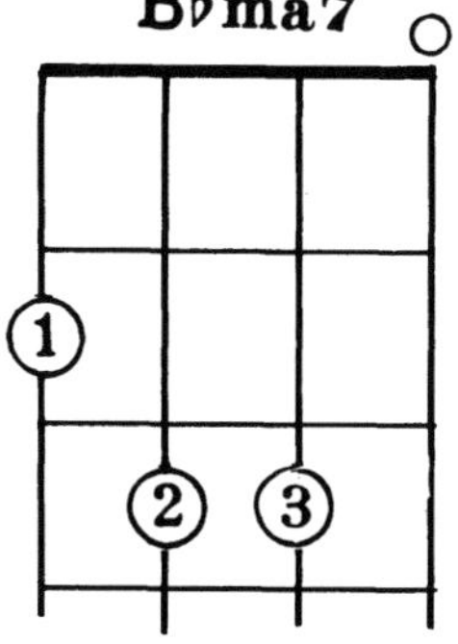

E♭ma7

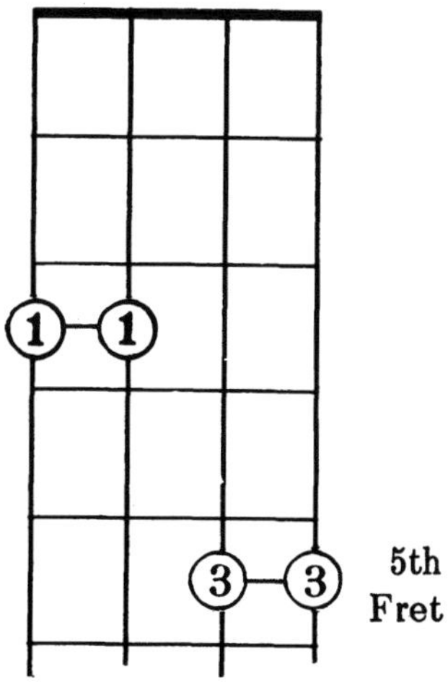

B♭ma7

5th Fret

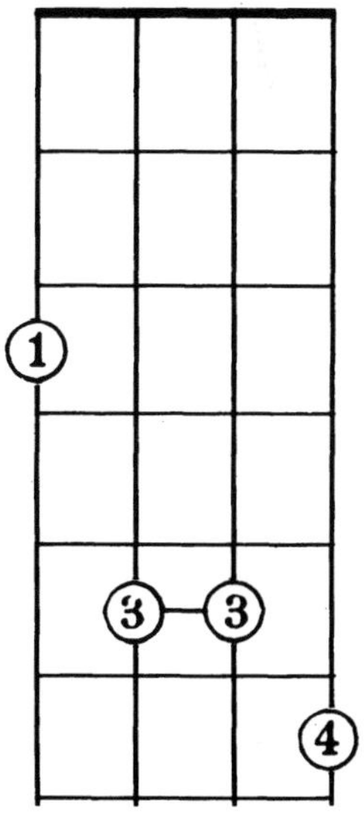

D♭ma7

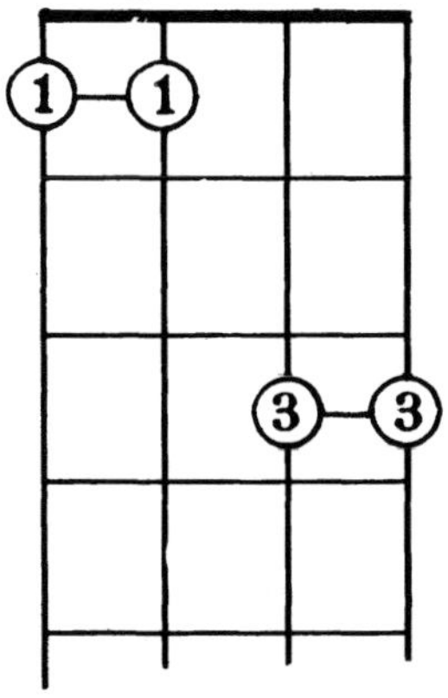

G♭ma7 & F♯ma7

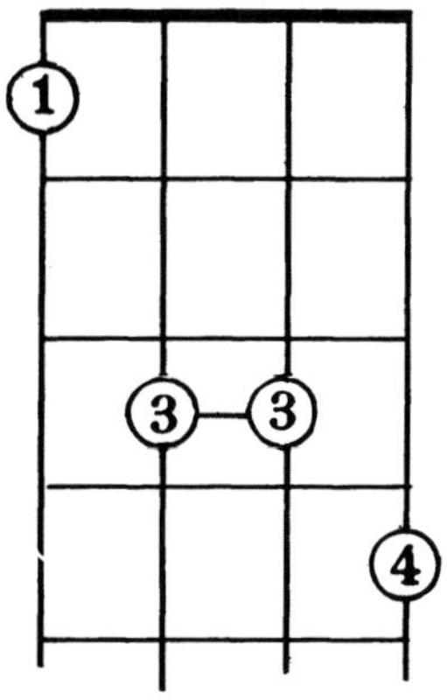

Bma7

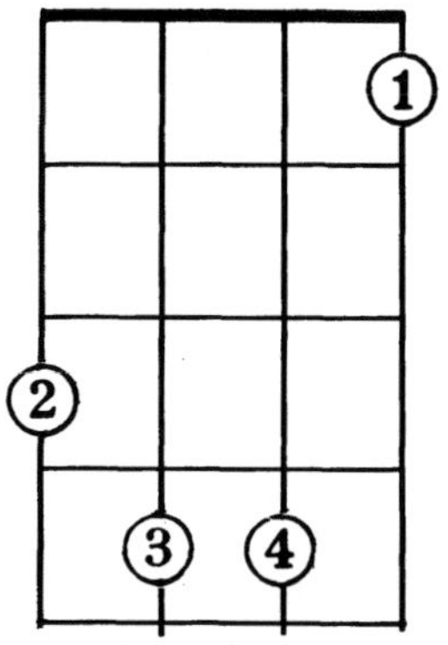

THE MINOR SEVENTH CHORDS

(m7 = Minor Seventh)

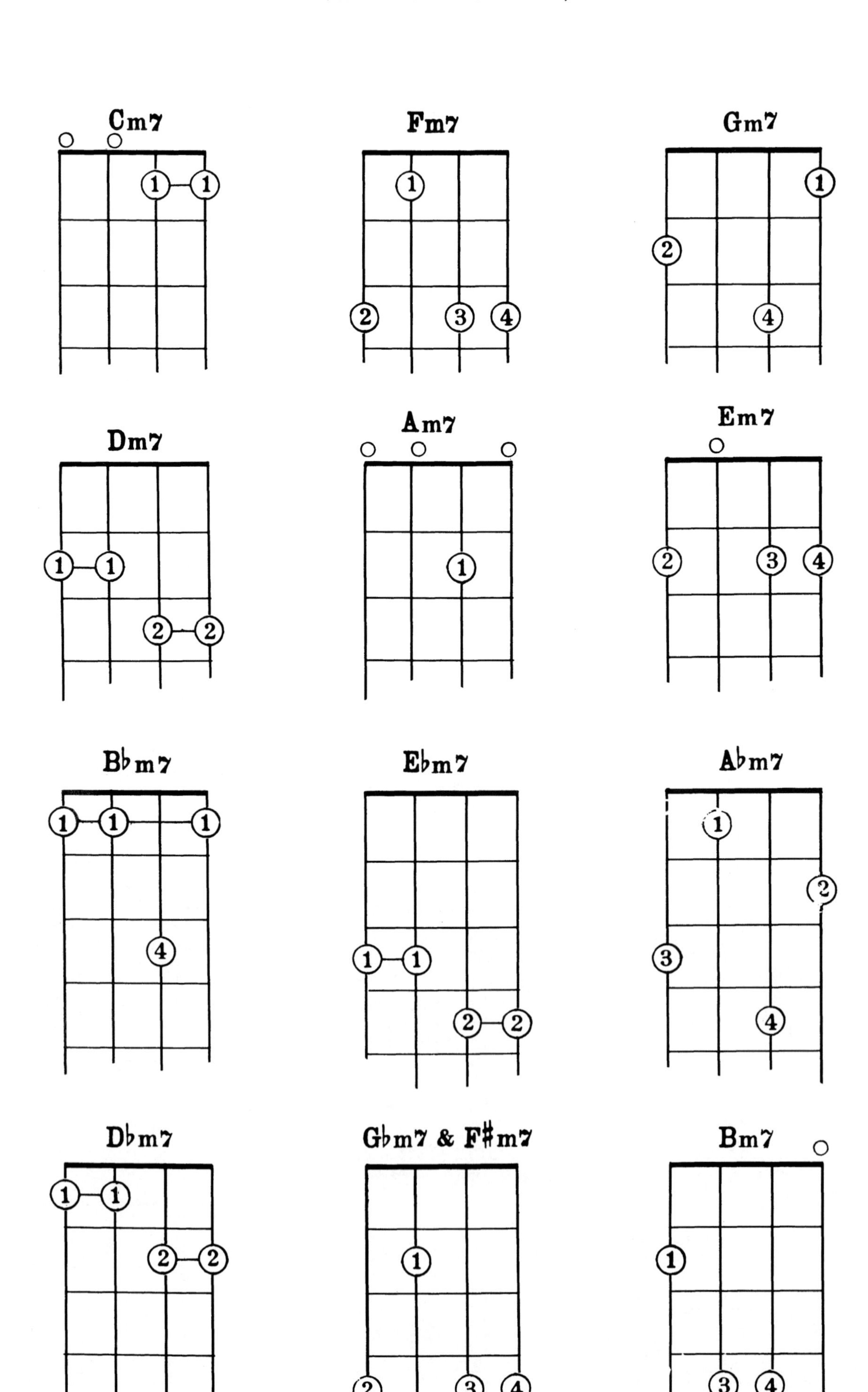

THE SIXTH CHORDS
(6 = Sixth)

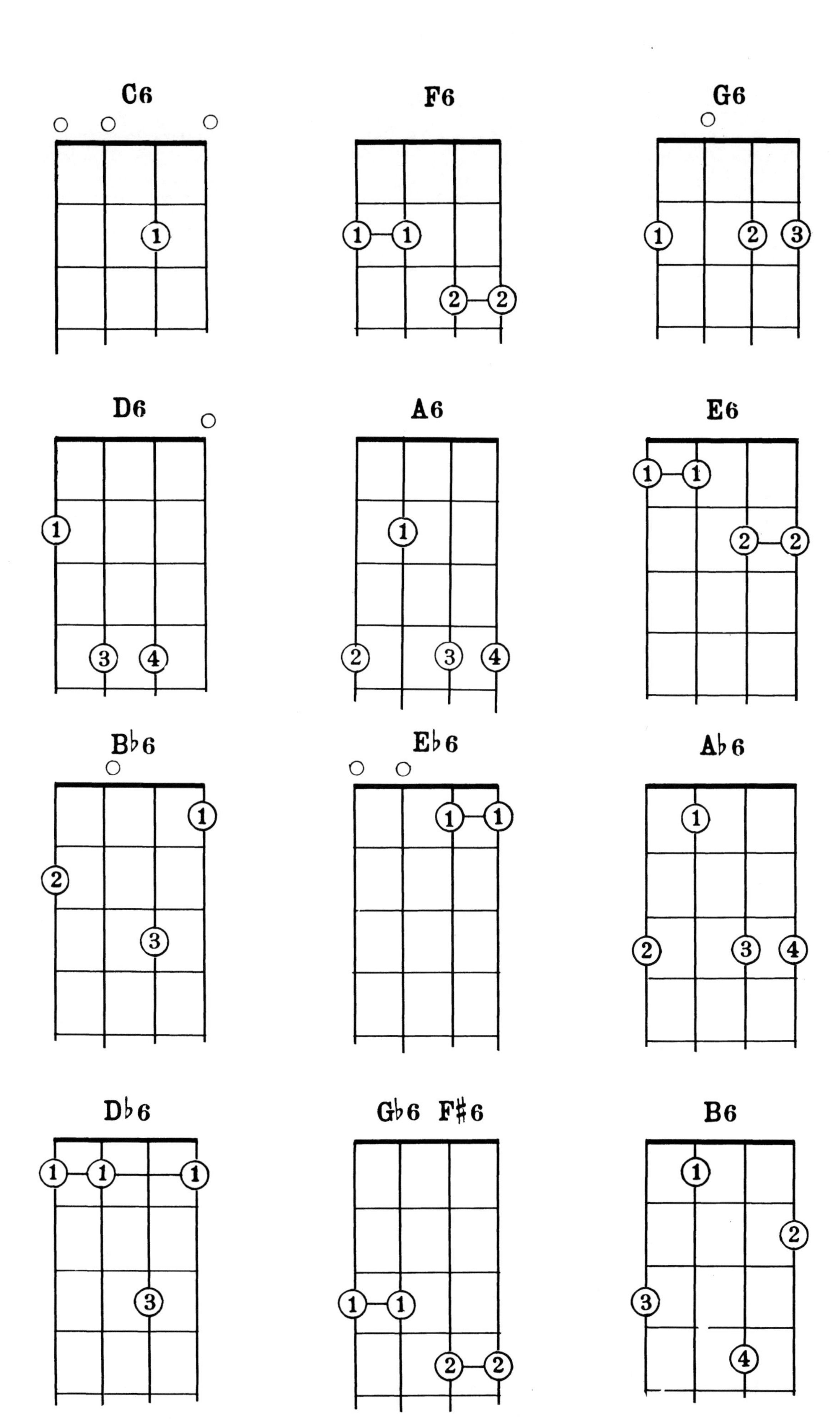

THE MINOR SIXTH CHORDS

(m6 = Minor Sixth)

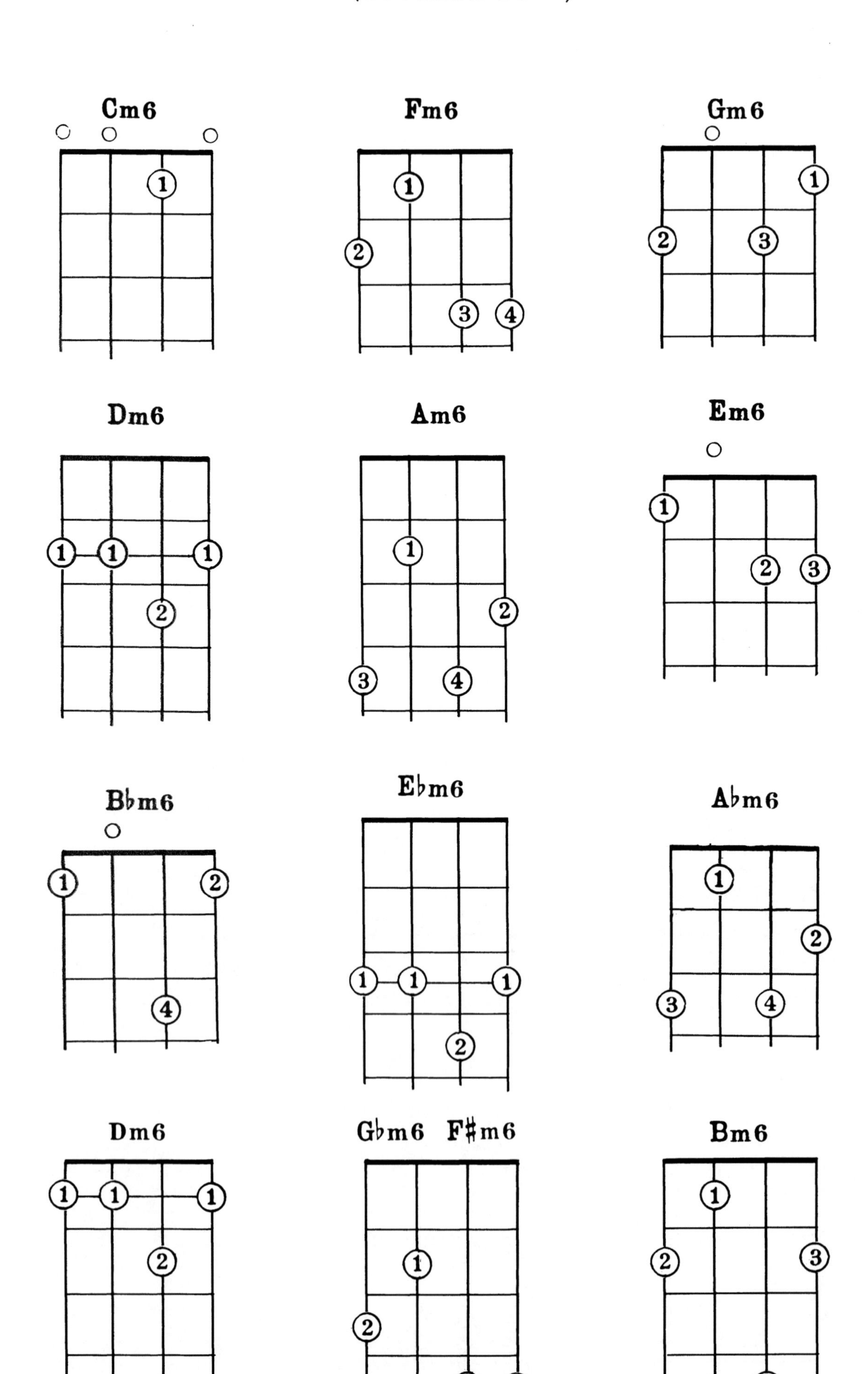

THE SEVENTH AUGMENTED FIFTH

(7+5)

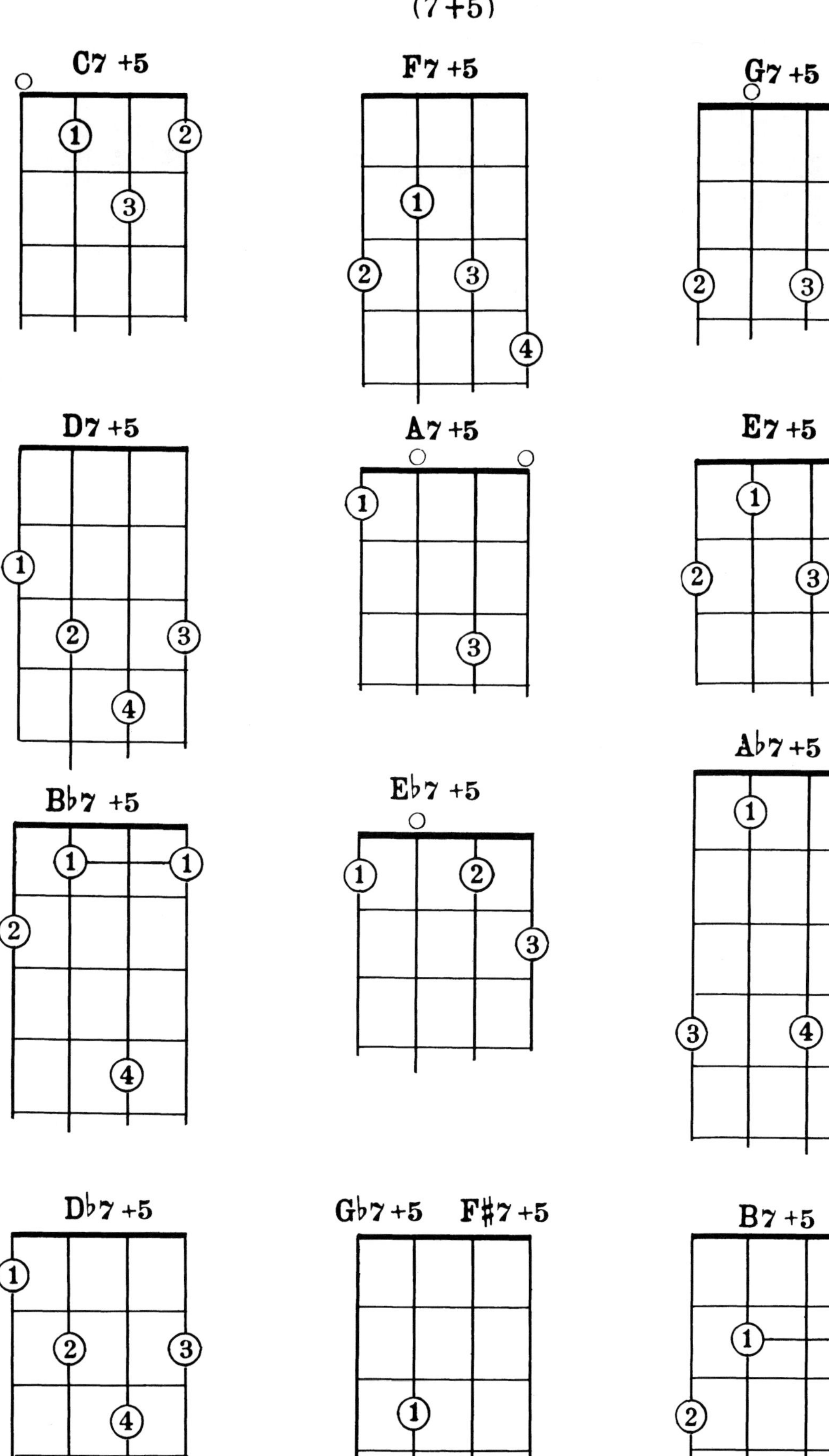

THE SEVENTH DIMINISHED FIFTH
(7 −5)

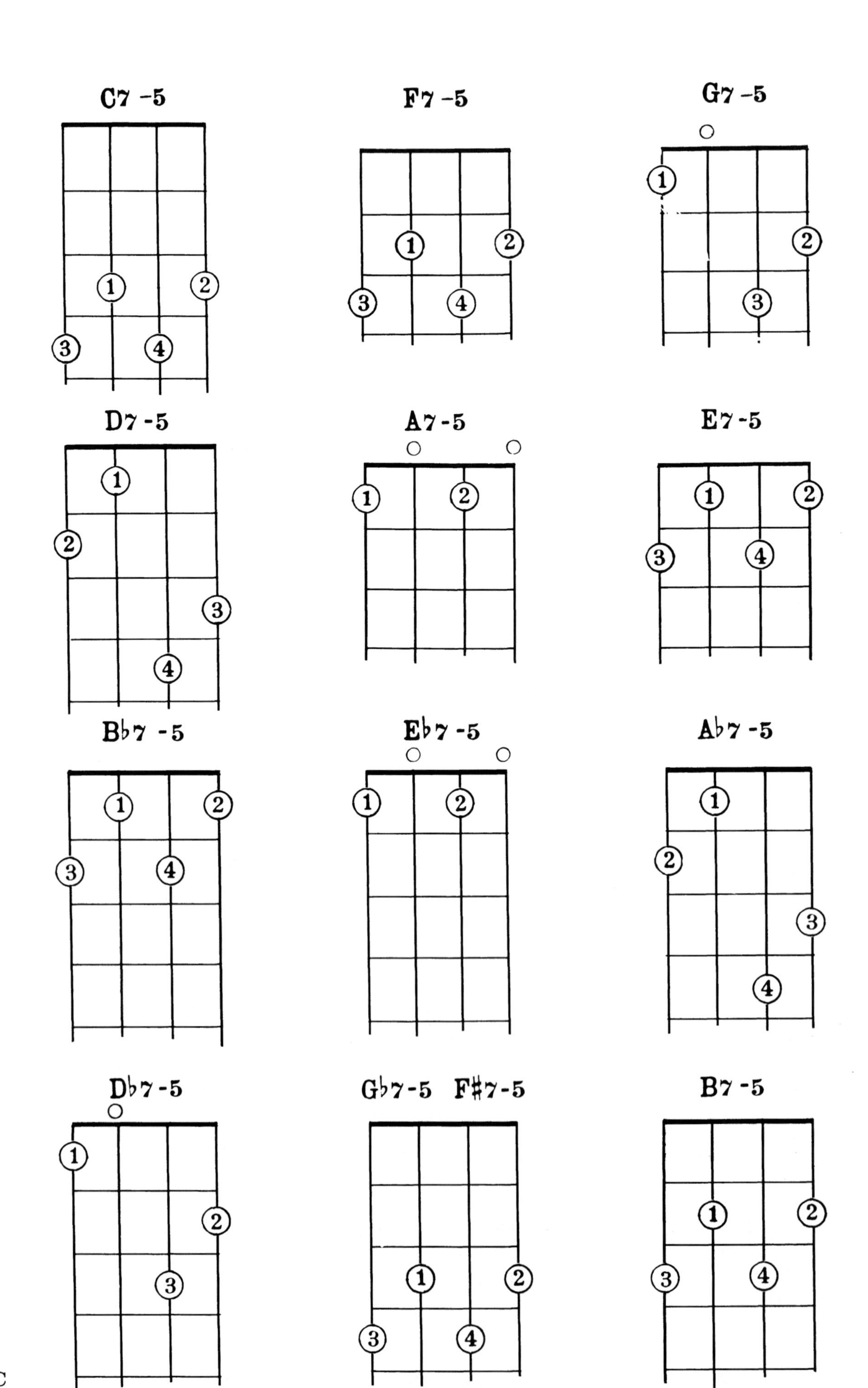

SUMMARY

The Major Chords

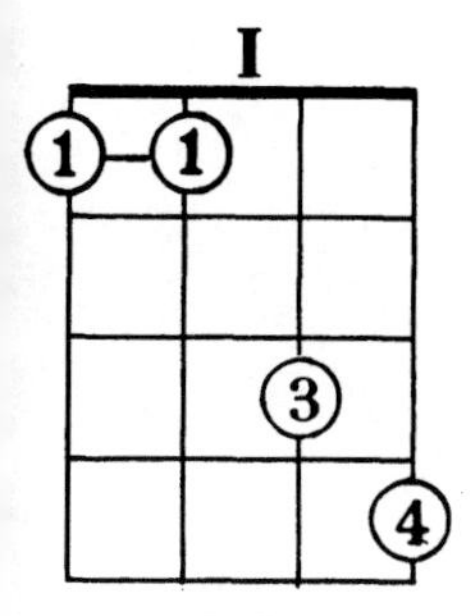

Frets	1	2	3	4	5	6	7	8	9	10	11	12
Chords	D♭	D	E♭	E	F	F♯ G♭	G	A♭	A	B♭	B	C

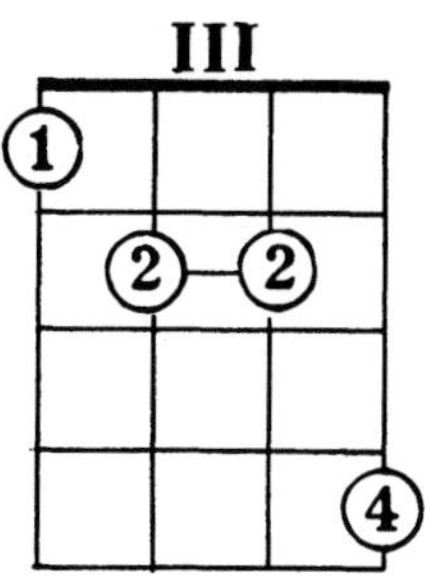

Frets	1	2	3	4	5	6	7	8	9	10	11	12
Chords	A	B♭	B	C	D♭ C♯	D	E♭	E	F	G♭ F♯	G	A♭

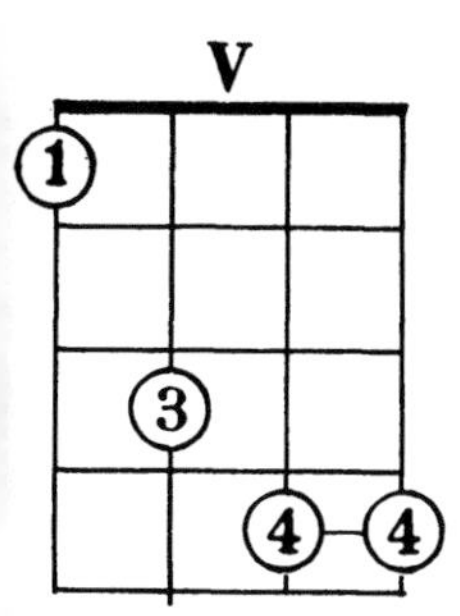

Frets	1	2	3	4	5	6	7	8	9	10	11	12
Chords	G♭ F♯	G	A♭	A	B♭	B	C	D♭ C♯	D	E♭	E	F

The Minor Chords

Im

Frets	1	2	3	4	5	6	7	8	9	10	11	12
Chords	D♭m	Dm	E♭m	Em	Fm	G♭m F♯m	Gm	A♭m	Am	B♭m	Bm	Cm

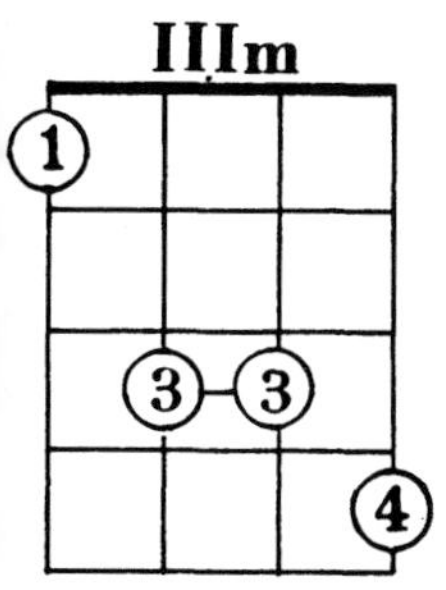

Frets	1	2	3	4	5	6	7	8	9	10	11	12
Chords	B♭m	Bm	Cm	D♭m C♯m	Dm	E♭m	Em	Fm	G♭m F♯m	Gm	A♭m	Am

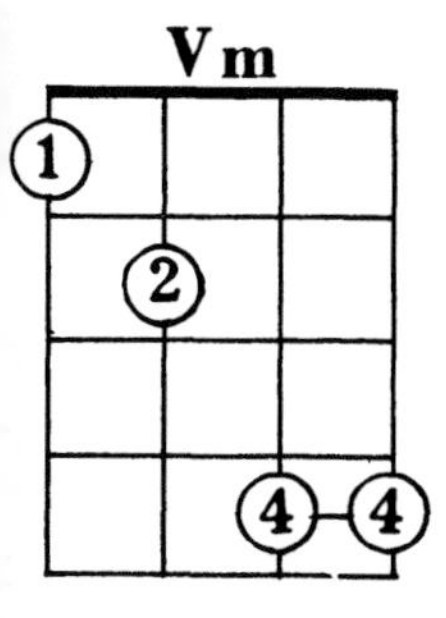

Frets	1	2	3	4	5	6	7	8	9	10	11	12
Chords	G♭m F♯m	Gm	A♭m	Am	B♭m	Bm	Cm	D♭m C♯m	Dm	E♭m	Em	Fm

THE SEVENTH CHORDS

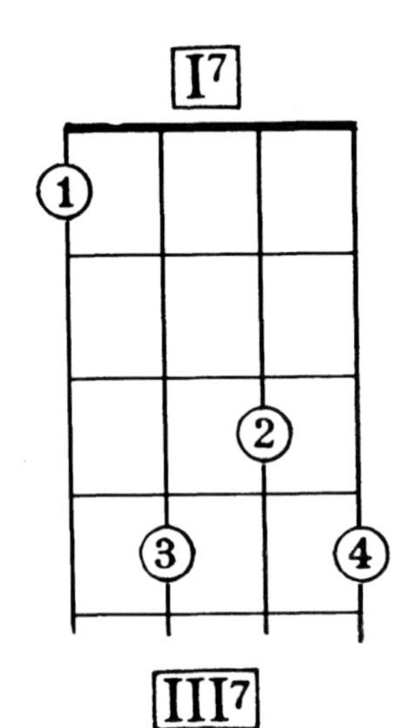

Frets	1	2	3	4	5	6	7	8	9	10	11	12
Chords	D♭7	D7	E♭7	E7	F7	G♭7 F♯7	G7	A♭7	A7	B♭7	B7	C7

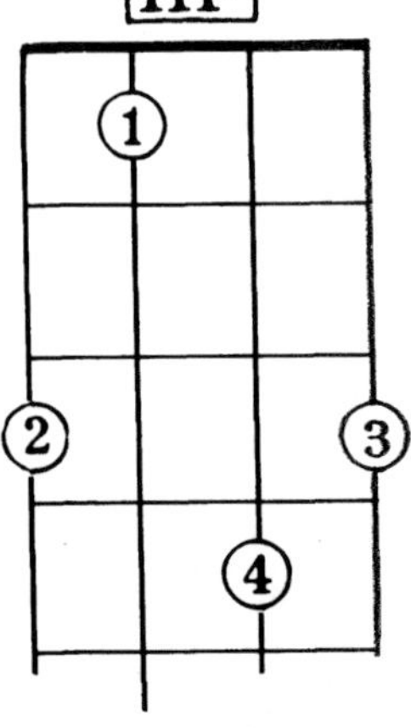

Frets	1	2	3	4	5	6	7	8	9	10	11	12
Chords	A♭7	A7	B♭7	B7	C7	D♭7 C♯7	D7	E♭7	E7	F7	G♭7 F♯7	G7

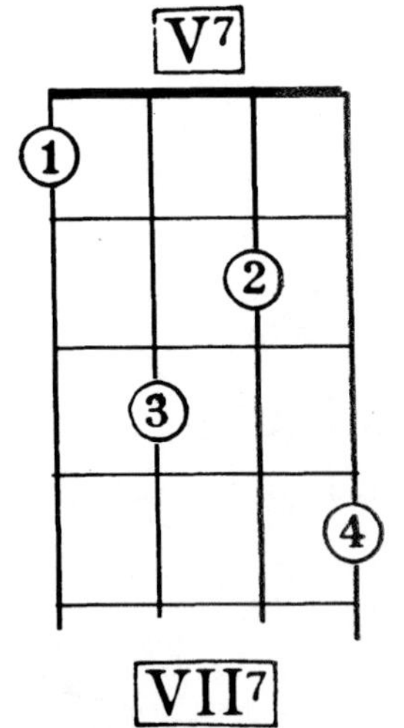

Frets	1	2	3	4	5	6	7	8	9	10	11	12
Chords	G♭7 F♯7	G7	A♭7	A7	B♭7	B7	C7	D♭7 C♯7	D7	E♭7	E7	F7

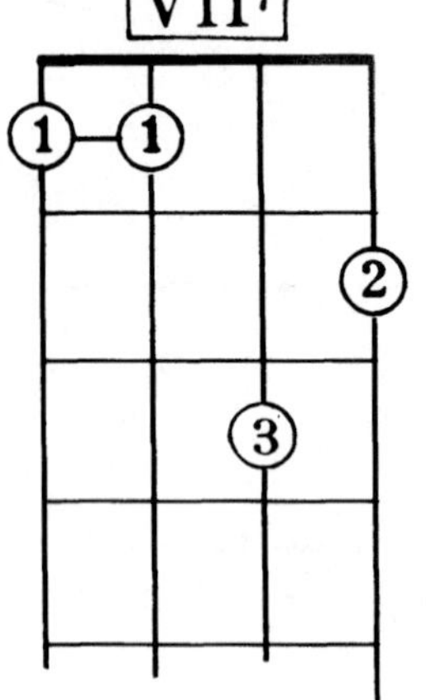

Frets	1	2	3	4	5	6	7	8	9	10	11	12
Chords	D♭7	D7	E♭7	E7	F7	G♭7 F♯7	G7	A♭7	A7	B♭7	B7	C7

THE ROMAN NUMERAL ABOVE THE FORM INDICATES THE CHORDAL TONE FOUND ON THE FIRST STRING.